VESTIGES

Illuminations: A Series on American Poetics

Series Editor, Jon Thompson

Illuminations focuses on the poetics and poetic practices of the contemporary moment in the USA. The series is particularly keen to promote a set of reflective works that include, but go beyond, traditional academic prose, so we take Walter Benjamin's rich, poetic essays published under the title of *Illuminations* as an example of the kind of approach we most value. Collectively, the titles published in this series aim to engage various audiences in a dialogue that will reimagine the field of contemporary American poetics. For more about the series, please visit its website at parlorpress.com/illuminations.

Books in the Series

Vestiges: Notes, Responses, and Essays 1988–2018 by Eric Pankey (2019)
Sudden Eden by Donald Revell (2019)
Prose Poetry and the City by Donna Stonecipher (2017)

VESTIGES

NOTES, RESPONSES, AND ESSAYS, 1988–2018

Eric Pankey

Parlor Press
Anderson, South Carolina
www.parlorpress.com

Parlor Press LLC, Anderson, South Carolina, USA
© 2019 by Parlor Press
Printed in the United States of America on acid-free paper.
    S A N: 2 5 4 - 8 8 7 9

        Library of Congress Cataloging-in-Publication Data on File

Illuminations
Series Editor: Jon Thompson

Cover art: " Chalk Lines," mixed media on Arches paper, Lisa Weiss. By
    kind and generous permission of the artist. http://www.lisaweiss.net
Interior and cover design: David Blakesley
Copyeditor: Jared Jameson

Parlor Press, LLC is an independent publisher of scholarly and trade
titles in print and multimedia formats. This book is available in paper,
cloth and eBook formats from Parlor Press on the World Wide Web at
http://www.parlorpress.com or through online and brick-and-mortar
bookstores. For submission information or to find out about Parlor Press
publications, write to Parlor Press, 3015 Brackenberry Drive, Anderson,
South Carolina, 29621, or email editor@parlorpress.com.

Contents

CONTENTS

Acknowledgments

Much of the work here appeared, often in earlier drafts, in the following online and print publications:

American Journal of Poetry
Boulevard
Chattahoochee Review
The Christian Century
The Christian Science Monitor
Colorado Review
Delmar
Free Verse
The Georgia Review
How a Poem Happens
Image
Interdisciplinary Studies
The Iowa Review
Manoa
The Mid-American Review
The Partisan Review
Pleiades
Poetry Daily
The Southern Review
UCity Review
The Writer's Chronicle

And in the following edited books:

Dark Horses: Poets on Overlooked Poems
Evensong: Contemporary American Poets on Spirituality
First Loves: Poets Introduce Essential Poems that Captivated and Inspired Them

The Radiant Lyre: Essays on Lyric Poetry
September 11, 2001: American Writers Respond
Until Everything is Continuous Again: American Poets on the Recent
    Work of W. S. Merwin

I am grateful to the generous attention of the editors of these publications for their invitation, insight, encouragement, and patience.

The essay "The Form of a Walk" was presented as part of a lecture series celebrating poets' birthdays at the Library of Congress. Thanks to Rob Casper for the invitation to discuss Robert Frost. "The Work of Poetry *or* An Imaginary Plane of Glass Parallel to Sea Level," was written upon an invitation from Jon Thompson at *Free Verse*.

Many works here had their beginnings as panel presentations at the annual Association of Writers and Writing Programs' conference and I thank the many members of the AWP staff, in particular David Fenza, Alycia Tessean, and Christian Teresi, who over the years have made the conference a lively and engaging gathering.

VESTIGES

1 To Repair the Material of Experience

Just as I am without one plea, *the choir sang. Those who knew the hymn sang out. I did not, but followed along in the hymnal.*

Against my will, I stepped out of the pew and into the aisle. Whatever had once filled my body pulled inward, and instead of growing denser, grew thin and vanished as it fell toward gravity. For an instant, I stood, unmoored, emptied, a hollow hull that all too suddenly filled to brimming with a flood, a charged and fluid weight from some other realm.

In between the emptying and the filling, I saw with absolute clarity a candor that is nothing but glare.

I carried what filled me as a burden to the pulpit. I stumbled, my eyes blurred by tears, my body racked with sobs. I cried, not out of joy or relief, but in mourning, in fear, and in wonder. This is Jesus's gift to you, my son, *the revivalist said. The feedback of his amplified voice rattled the windows. Dozens of others followed me down the aisle.*

A man and a woman ushered me behind the choir stall through a door to a hallway. There in the hallway they asked me to kneel, and when I would not or could not, they kneeled and prayed. The man buried his face in his fists. The woman held her arms up, her palms open to the sky, as one might to a sudden downpour. I stood, my head lowered, my shoulders hunched with weeping, as they thanked the Lord for saving me.

The hall light above us, reflected in the newly waxed floor, seemed doubled in brightness, and all I could see, with my eyes half-shut, was a crown of fire, its spikes of light smudged by my tears.

By then the choir was well into the benediction:

'Twas grace that taught my heart to fear,
And grace my fears relieved;
How precious did that grace appear
The hour I first believed.

That night, alone in my room, I tried to pray. I read in the Bible they had given me. The words of Jesus, printed in red, were the hardest to read in the dim light of my bedroom. Although the sun had set, across the street the thud of a basketball continued against a backboard for a half-hour. A dog howled. Cicadas started in. The mundane seemed a great comfort.

How much time passed I cannot remember, but I had not given up reading. The room turned cold suddenly and unnaturally. The air pressure dropped. I breathed the chilly, thin air, but with difficulty. In the room's four corners, a pale, sourceless smoke swirled slowly, swirled into unbodied icy forms, that fell one at a time like fists upon me. They struck me from all sides.

They hailed down without mercy and without a single word. I could hear the whip of their plummet, the air closing back on itself, my own voice, a mumble of prayer. They weighed me down and pressed me, stone by stone, until I bore their glacial mass as my own.

Were they what I had lost, or were they more of what had filled me as I had walked down the aisle? In a moment such as this, one expects, but cannot demand an answer.

A whole night passed. I breathed the steamy air of morning. I found whatever they were—demons, ghosts, angels—gone. Despite the crush and the rasp, the abrasion of their touch, I felt my body whole. But I knew nothing about the condition of my soul.

: :

Never since then has that realm of the Spirit, for lack of a better name, made itself known to me again. I am like the man Flannery O'Connor describes in her essay, "Novelist and Believer," who "can neither believe nor contain himself in disbelief and who searches desperately, feeling about in all experience for the lost God" (167).

One night as young man I had seen the Spirit. I could not help but believe it, possessed as I was of it. Once it vanished from my sight, I could not believe nor disbelieve it. Worse, I could not bury the memory, nor shake it free.

"It is strange," Emily Dickinson writes in a letter from 1877, "that the most intangible things are the most adhesive" (589).

: :

More and more, the contents of my own poems have become those of a spiritual crisis: the troubled existence of one balancing on the narrow threshold between faith and doubt. I do not see myself as a "religious poet," and yet I long to write about, as O'Connor puts it, "people in a world where something is obviously lacking, where there is the general mystery of incompleteness . . ." (134).

My attempt as a poet is not to elaborate the realm of the soul, but to elucidate it, to somehow (with words of all things) grind a lens that just might magnify and focus the soul's immanence. The difficulty of such an attempt is this: to be magnified and focused, a thing must be seen, or at least located. For all the talk of the spirit and the soul, what I am addressing here is the usual business of poetry—the attempt through the medium of language to make an absence present.

For me that night, contact with the soul was a bodily experience and, as a result, is understood best not as a metaphysical awareness, but as carnal knowledge. Thus, words, a means made in the body, seem an appropriate vehicle to an end—that is, to a confrontation with the spiritual. "Between the usual subjects of poetry," T.S. Eliot writes in a letter from 1930, "and 'devotional verse' there is a . . . field very much unexplored by modern poets, the experience of the man in search of God, and trying to explain to himself his intenser human feelings in terms of the divine goal . . ." (288). And though the questions seem here primarily theological (What is the divine? How is it made manifest? Where does it reside?), writing becomes a way, an expanse that bridges the known and the unknown, and as Eliot writes about George Herbert, that bridges "despair and bliss," "agitation and serenity" (25).

: :

If, as Wallace Stevens says in his "Adagia," "Poetry is a means of redemption" (186), one must wonder for whom—the poet? The reader? And what is it that such writing can recover, deliver, buy back, or save? Stevens answers by not answering these questions, when he says: "The final belief is to believe in a fiction, which you know is a fiction, there being nothing else. The exquisite truth is to know that it is a fiction and you believe it willingly" (189). I would argue that Stevens, a religiously faithful agnostic, is one of our great spiritual poets, wrestling with the same issues as believers, but from the other corner of the ring. It seems fitting to answer my questions of poetry's redemptive powers with a passage from Stevens' teacher George Santayana, who writes in the final chapter of *Interpretations of Poetry and Religion*, "The great function of poetry . . . is precisely this: to repair the material of experience . . . and then out of that living but indefinite material to build new structures, richer, finer, fitter to the primary tendencies of our nature, truer to the ultimate possibilities of the soul" (207).

: :

To repair the material of experience. What else is redemption? Poetry's force *is* revelatory, and such a force is achieved by descending into the physical, into materiality, until the *thinginess* of the thing is indecipherable from its essence, and its essence from its *thinginess*, and, for once, the thing is seen as whole.

: :

To redeem suggests an exchange. Poetry is a mode through which exchange is made, a mode of experience through which the world is transformed, and is, to use a word weighted with spiritual implications, transfigured. A writer with a spiritual sensibility must remember that an encounter with a god is, as O'Connor asserts, both a "natural and supernatural experience," and as such, it must be transformed in such a way as to be "understandable and credible to. . .[the] reader" (161).

Writing about Eliot as a "Christian" poet, Vincent Buckley says that such a poet, "is not [a poet] declaring, nor [a poet] puzzling, but [a poet] wondering; and in his wonder capable of torment as much as joy" (222). Work that might be called work of "devotion" can be work that is questioning, confrontational, and challenging to whatever rules the Spirit. If the business of the poet is to wonder, then language is the means of such wonder. Language is, in the end, the only means to any end for a poet. It is the means of transport. If we call Eliot or George Herbert spiritual poets we suggest that their language is, as Santayana puts it, the work of "private imagination[s]" recreating the religion afresh.

: :

In his 1987 film, *Wings of Desire*, Wim Wenders shows us two angels sitting in the front seat of a BMW in a car dealer's showroom. These two angels have been observing and recording the lives of Berliners. At times, but rarely, they have intervened. One of the angels, Damiel, longs to abandon his spiritual realm and enter the world of the material.

What he says from the front seat of the BMW seems for me an apt *ars poetica*, because the angel's longing for the earthly (the English subtitles making what he says a lovely poem in free verse lines) mirrors my own homesickness, my own mundane longing for a once-known realm of the spirit:

> It's great to live only by the spirit,
> to testify day by day for eternity
> only to the spiritual side of people,
> but sometimes I get fed up with my spiritual existence.
> Instead of forever hovering above,
> I'd like to feel there's some weight to me,
> to end my eternity and bind me to the earth.
> At each step, each gust of wind,
> I'd like to be able to say, "Now, now, now,"
> and no longer say "since always" and "forever."
> To sit in an empty seat at a card table,
> and be greeted, if only by a nod. . . .
> Not that I want to beget a child
> or plant a tree right away,
> but it would be quite something to come in
> after a long day like Phillip Marlowe
> and feed the cat, to have a fever,
> to have blackened fingers from the newspaper,
> to be excited not only by the mind
> but at last by a meal, the curve of a neck,

by a ear. To lie! Through the teeth.
To feel your skeleton moving along as you walk.
Finally to suspect instead of forever knowing.
To be able to say "Ah" and "Oh" and "Hey"
instead of "Yes" and "Amen."

Damiel's longing is both understandable and credible, and for
a writer who might wish to confront spiritual concerns through
the vehicle of writing, it is, as well, instructive. Faith, at least in
my experience of it, *is* to finally suspect, "To be able to say 'Ah'
and 'Oh' . . . instead of 'Yes' and 'Amen.'" To be surprised by
detail, to see in "the curve of a neck" both the natural and the
supernatural. "Miracles," Santayana writes in *The Idea of Christ in
the Gospels or God in Man*, "are so called because they excite wonder. . . . The essence of miracle is that, in breaking through
the superficial routine of events, it manifests the real power
that brings them about, and proves this power is profoundly
human" (80).

: :

"They are religious, except me," Dickinson, in a letter from
1862, writes about her family, "and address an eclipse, every
morning, whom they call their 'Father'" (404).

That image of an eclipse captures the complexity and
mystery of both the incompleteness and the absence that the act
of writing attempts to complete and fill. What can we know of a
thing we have been told we can no longer safely look upon, that
we can know only by looking at its shadow concentrated and
cast through a pinhole?

If the strange memoir that opens this essay were titled
"Parable," what exegesis might be offered? Is it a confession of
a faith? Is it a tale meant to provoke one's disbelief? Is its witness meant to be trusted? A fiction is as close as I can come to
reclaiming the mystery and strangeness of that night so many
years ago when I felt the thing I now call my soul transfigured.
The story I told is the story I tell and in telling reshape: a fiction that is both its own reality and an approximation of what
we call *reality*.

John Donne, in a sermon from 1626, offers a figure that accurately embodies the paradox of how a fiction allows us to know the unknowable:

> A Compasse is a necessary thing in a Ship, and the helpe of that Compasse brings the Ship home safe, and yet the compasse hath some variations, it doth not looke directly north; Neither is that starre which we call the North-pole, or by which we know the North-pole, the very pole itself; but we call it so, and we make our uses of it, and our conclusions by it, as if it were so, because it is the nearest starre to that Pole. (523)

2 Silences and Forgeries

Western wind, when wilt thou blow,
The small rain down can rain?
Christ, if my love were in my arms
And I in my bed again!

What binding material holds the first two lines of this poem to the final two lines? Certainly, we are pulled on by meter and rhyme, rhythmic and melodic conventions that create expectation and offer fulfillment. I would like to argue, however, that the poem's felt emotion is not only in the language, as precise and lovely as it is, but in the unspoken transition between the poem's two halves. Something quite magical happens between lines two and three.

The poem balances on a pinpoint of silence. No spoken rhetorical argument adheres lines one and two to lines three and four. At the center of the poem, what is left unsaid, what is unsayable, is where the reader somehow recognizes and knows the complete truth of the poem. This silence is not only a silence between notes, between the noted, not only a silence that is conjunction, but is the unutterable that asserts the poem's argument, the unutterable that is the essence of the poem.

: :

There is a story in Luke's gospel, near the end, in chapter 24 verses 13-35 of the Revised Standard Version of the Bible, after the execution of Jesus and the early accounts of his resurrection, that goes like this:

That very day two of them were going to a village named Emmaus, about seven miles from Jerusalem, and talking about these things that had happened. While they were talking together, Jesus himself drew near and went with them. But their eyes were kept from recognizing him. And he said to them, "What is this conversation which thou art holding with each other as you walk?" And they stood still looking sad. Then one of them named Cleopas, answered him, "Are you the only visitor to Jerusalem who does not know the things that have happened there in these days?" And he said to them, "What things?" And they said to him, "Concerning Jesus of Nazareth, who was a prophet mighty in deed and word before God and all people, and how our chief priests and rulers delivered him up to be condemned to death and crucified him. But we had hoped that he was the one to redeem Israel. Yes, and besides all this some women of our company amazed us. They were at the tomb early in the morning and did not find his body; and they came back saying that they had even seen a vision of angels, who said he was alive. Some of those who were with us went to the tomb and found it just as the women had said; but him they did not see." And he said to them, "O foolish men, and slow of heart to believe all the prophets have spoken! Was it not necessary that Christ should suffer these things and enter into his glory?" And beginning with Moses and all the prophets he interpreted to them all scripture concerning himself. So they drew near to the village to which they were going. He appeared to be going further, but they constrained him, saying, "Stay with us, for it is toward evening and day is now far spent." So he went inside with them. When he was at the table with them, he took bread and blessed it, and broke it, and gave it to them. And their eyes were opened and they recognized him; and he vanished out of their sight .

When I was a boy I spent much of my time looking at art history books at the library. I liked narrative paintings over a still life or landscape. Although I did not have a religious upbringing, I found myself most fascinated with paintings depicting scenes from the Gospels. The story of the supper at Emmaus was taught to me first by a painting. I knew then little of the narrative, the story just told, but I knew the essence of the moment the painting attempts to capture—that moment after Christ breaks the bread *and* the disciples' eyes are opened *and* what they are opened to vanishes *and* is lost to them. All of course (and this is most important) in the same instant. Anyone reading the painting would know of the disciples' astonishment, of their recognition and disbelief. The moment the painting depicts balances on a precarious edge, and the moment after the moment of the painting tips into another reality. All this I knew from the painting, but how?

: :

I found the painting in a Time-Life Library of Art volume called *The World of Vermeer*. The painting, *Christ and the Disciples at Emmaus*, is not a Vermeer, but a forgery of Vermeer by Hans Van Meegeren. The composition of the forgery borrows freely from a painting of less dubious origin, Carravaggio's *Supper at Emmaus*. As in many narrative paintings of religious content, content such as *The Annunciation*, the *Conversion of St. Paul on the Road to Damascus*, the *Nativity*, both Carravaggio's and Van Meegeren's versions of the Emmaus story attempt to capture a moment not so much of narration, but a moment of spiritual perception, of precise understanding, of clear epiphany. To do so, however, the painters cheat.

They offer the recognizable Christ, the broken bread, and the disciples' opened eyes. But the moment of perception, what we might call here and in "Western Wind" the *lyric moment*, is not reproduced. The moment of seeing is the exact moment when the seen disappears. The painters' materials cannot reproduce such sleight of hand, and yet those inadequate materials do produce the sensation of the moment, a moment of *between-ness*.

: :

Because of language's inadequacies we always speak inexactly, failing always, as we often say, to say what we mean. Still, amid the misrepresentation that any word offers, we possess some inkling, some glimpse of the reality of the thing. "Reality," Wallace Stevens says, "is not what is. It consists of the many realities it can be made into" (202). That *into* is where the silent lyric moment takes us.

: :

Those two travelers on the road to Emmaus find themselves at a border between doubt and faith. Until the lyric moment of their recognition, they walk along that border as along the border between two countries equally difficult to inhabit. That third traveler "appeared to be going further" but is constrained and stays with them. The two disciples talk, but their talk does not lead them to understanding. Their talk circles the truth. It is only in their silence, as John Drury tells us in his commentary on Luke that "The two are left to tumble to the truth of everything" (425).

: :

The lyric poem is often a text of dubious authority because it attempts to make the moment momentous, to bear witness to that which only the poet has witnessed. But in the hands of the best poets the lyric poem leads us to a visionary threshold that is crossed:

God's Grandeur

The world is charged with the grandeur of God.
    It will flame out, like shining from shook foil;
    It gathers to a greatness, like the ooze of oil
Crushed. Why do men then now not reck his rod?
Generations have trod, have trod, have trod;
    And all is seared with trade; bleared, smeared with toil;
    And wears man's smudge and shares man's smell: the soil
Is bare now, nor can foot feel, being shod.
And for all this, nature is never spent;

    There lives the dearest freshness deep down things;

And through the last light of black West went
  Oh, morning, at the brown brink eastward, springs—
Because the Holy Ghost over the bent
  World broods with warm breast and with ah! bright
    wings. (lines 1-14)

Certainly, silence does not reign here. Like some dense planet with outrageous gravity, this poem by Gerard Manley Hopkins pulls us more and more into its orbit until we collide hard
against it surface. All the argument of this sonnet, all the well-
wrought (some have said *overwrought*) rhyme of the poem, all the
matter of the poem is drawn inward until the poem implodes
with the mere utterance: *ah!* Here where the poem hesitates,
here where the poem is least word-crazed, is the gap through
which we too witness the visionary, the lyric instance and insistence of the poem.

: :

In *Poetics of Music*, Stravinsky writes, "All creation presupposes at
its origin a sort of appetite that is brought on by the foretaste of
discovery. This foretaste of the creative act accompanies the in-
tuitive grasp of an unknown entity already possessed but not yet
intelligible. . ." (51). The moment of a lyric—this small thing I
am attempting to define—is when the possessed unknown entity becomes intelligible and felt.

: :

At the moment of recognition, the Emmaus disciples know,
in retrospect, all their eyes have been closed to, all that has
naggingly haunted them, all they have gained and lost. For all
its darkness, "God's Grandeur" collapses into joy and praise.
How does the unknown entity become intelligible in the lyric moment? It is the language's imperfections that allow the
not-yet-intelligible to be glimpsed. Those imperfections often
show themselves on the surface of poems as gaps, as *O* or *Ah!*, as
a dash, as a white space, as syntactical ambiguity, as an absence
of conjunction or other sorts of rhetorical connective tissue.

: :

14

ERIC PANKEY

"It is not important that they survive," Wallace Stevens writes about his poems in the late poem, "The Planet on the Table":

> What mattered was that they should bear
> Some lineament or character,
>
> Some affluence, if only half-perceived,
> In the poverty of their words,
> Of the planet of which they were part (line 11-15).

Lyric poems can be little miracles: impoverished words creating worlds of Beauty and Truth. We recognize (to make a noun out of Stravinsky's definition) our *intuitive-but-not-yet-intelligible-grasp-of-something-already-owned-but-still-not-known* because the poet's words and silences, as flawed as they might be, remind us of our ownership of what we have not yet held. The inadequate language of the lyric, nevertheless, takes us to the brink of knowing.

: :

The following poem by Emily Dickinson, like so many lyric poems, emanates a seemingly sourceless light. We are drawn to it, not so much seeking its source, but to be illuminated by it:

> Mine—by the Right of White Election!
> Mine—by the Royal Seal!
> Mine—by the Sign of Scarlet Prison--
> Bars—cannot conceal!
>
> Mine—here—in Vision—and in Veto!
> Mine—by the Grave's Repeal—
> Titled—Confirmed—
> Delirious Charter!
> Mine—long as Ages steal (lines 1-9)!

In this halting, darkly joyous poem, it is easy to see that one of the businesses of poetry is celebration. Just what is being celebrated, what is *owned* in the poem is the difficulty of explication. But deciphering is not what the poem itself calls for. In fact, it resists paraphrase. Lyrics work often like riddles: the very language that defers meaning is the very language that reveals meaning. The distance the poem places before us is not dissatisfying, unpleasant, or merely clever. It asks us to see in ways and from vantage points we have not known before. We are not invited to find the poem's solution as we are in a riddle, but we are invited to experience and feel the sense and mystery of its language.

: :

In that painting by Van Meegeren, (a forgery that was believed for eight years to be a master work of Vermeer's and only uncovered as a forgery by the forger's own confession. He was being charged with collaborating with the Nazis for selling them Dutch art treasures, his own forgeries) although there is light entering through the window at the right of Christ, Christ himself seems to be the source of light, illuminating the quarter-moon of the disciple's face whose back is turned to us, illuminating the profile of the disciple who holds the table tightly at its edge as if the source of light has disappeared already. Van Meegeren painted the entire forgery on top of a seventeenth century canvas, and since some of the white paint from the original could not be removed, Van Meegeren built his entire composition around that which persisted to show through.

: :

While a lyric may be riddled with gaps and silences, those breaches and imperfections are what lead the reader to look for connectedness, because connectedness is the habit of poetry. I say *look*, but more exactly, the reader trusts that there will be wholeness, trusts that the parts (even the missing parts of the poem's world) equal a whole world. *Christ and the Disciples at Emmaus*, forgery or not, moved me when I first saw it. The painting offers us the complete density of a moment; it offers the present tense as a fulcrum on which the weight of history and vision balances, tipping dangerously, it seems, this way, dangerously that way. It offers us a present tense we can never quite know in this world: a gravity that holds things together by holding them apart.

3 The Word

The Word is and is without advent. As a body is a grave, so too is a word.

: :

Do we through words remove ourselves from, or attach ourselves to, the otherness we name?

: :

The given, often in these discussions, is that we live in an era *after* belief—one where god's death is not as yet another myth about the god, but historical fact. I am not sure I begin at the given. After the death of god, the god goes on living as god, called forth, as before, by words.

: :

Words do not veil but reveal. Words do not reveal but veil.

: :

In the beginning was the Word, and all the following words are embellishments upon the Word.

: :

In the beginning was the Word, and all the following words are splinters of that Word.

: :

Some poets want words to be transparent, to illuminate. Some poets want words to be impenetrable, to obscure. Many believers approach the Word in the same way.

: :

We know the world as a translation.

4 A Forgotten Language

A bsence (and the finding of a language to embody it) is and
has been a recurring concern in W. S. Merwin's poetry.
In *The Rain in the Trees*, we find that the very words that once gave
shape to the missing, the lost, and the extinct are themselves
endangered. In "Witness," Merwin writes:

> I want to tell what the forests
> were like
> I will have to speak
> in a forgotten language (lines 1-4)

The poet faces a double crisis. The only way to communicate
the existence of a thing now threatened and on the verge of extinction is a "forgotten" language, perhaps an archaic, obsolete
language, a dead language, or a language, like the forest itself,
already almost vanished. Another possible reading is that this
"forgotten language" is an occult and hermetic language that
the poet can speak but few who listen can decipher and understand. Either way, the witness of this poem is the articulation
of the desire to bear witness. The poem offers a somewhat de-
feated admission that the words to do so may not wholly communicate. Throughout *The Rain in the Trees*, the poet attempts to
wrap language around the central irritant of loss, around the
complexity and paradox of absence and its dogged ineffability.
The poet hears and knows an arcane language and is burdened
to translate it, to witness to those who cannot access and understand it.

In the poem "Utterance," Merwin speaks to the poet's role as a conduit and medium between the ancient and sacred and the present tense of the quotidian and mundane:

Sitting over words
very late I have heard a kind of whispered sighing
not far
like a night wind in pines or like the sea in the dark
the echo of everything that has ever
been spoken
still spinning its one syllable
between the earth and silence (1-8)

Here the absent language must be courted, conjured, by way of words. By "sitting over words" during the late hour, the poet can listen for and hear the "sigh" and "echo of everything that has ever / been spoken" (lines 5-6). In "Utterance," the manner is mystical, with the poet admitting to a sensitive antenna that can pick up all the frequencies "between earth and silence" (line 8), between the heard and unheard, as a single syllable.

Loss is Merwin's subject in *The Rain in the Trees*. The losses range from the intimate to the global, from a personal memory flickering out to the colonial destruction of an indigenous culture to the extinction of whole species. His conventional mode throughout the book is elegiac, but the poems mourn and lament the loss of much more than individual humans, although the loss of his parents, the receding distance of childhood, and a nostalgia for a past home give shape to many poems here. Here his words are not the garments of what he will never be. Instead, he uses language to bridge the gaps between the known and the as-yet-unknown, between what one can articulate and what one has felt, between diurnal and geologic time, between the moment and the mythic, as in "Losing a Language":

A breath leaves the sentences and does not come back
yet the old still remember something that they could say

but they know now that such things are no longer believed
and the young have fewer words

many of the things the words were about
no longer exist

the noun for standing in mist by a haunted tree
the verb for I (line 1-8)

In an intimate poem, "The First Year," knowledge and language unhinge from one another:

When the words had all been used
for other things
we saw the first day begin

out of the calling water
and the black branches
leaves no bigger than your fingertips
were unfolding on the tree of heaven
against the old stained wall
their green sunlight
that had never shone before

waking together we were the first
to see them
and we knew them then

all languages were foreign and the first
year rose (lines 1-15)

The speaker and the beloved find gnosis when words have "all
been used." Only then does time begin in this Edenic (or is
it post-Edenic?) realm. Their insight and knowledge are
theirs only in a realm of the ineffable where "all the languages"
are "foreign."

In a wholly original elegy for John Keats, "Chord,"
Keats's short life is written as parallel to the ecology and history of Hawai'i at the same moment: "While Keats wrote they
were cutting down the sandalwood forests," the poem begins,
and it ends with another lamentation for a damaged language
and culture:

while he coughed they carried the trunks to the hole in
     the forest the size of a foreign ship
while he groaned on the voyage to Italy they fell on the
     trails and were broken
when he lay with the odes behind him the wood was sold
     for cannons
when he lay watching the window they came home and
     lay down
and an age arrived when everything was explained in an-
     other language (lines 11-15)

Questions about language riddle Merwin's work. In "Losing a Language," for instance, the loss equals the loss of knowledge, culture, and understanding, while in "The First Year," language must be exhausted and set aside in order to achieve vision and insight. Are we to imagine Keats's short life and small body of work equal to the felling of a sandalwood forest, that the triumph of the language of Keats's poems is somehow implicated in the arrival of an age in Hawai'i "when everything was explained in another language (line 15)"?

Merwin's poems in *The Rain in the Trees* tend to ask more questions than they answer. They rise out of a silence as if out of an aftermath. Their drama is often offstage. Or they rely on lyric convention, such as a poem of travel and leave-taking. In "Travelling Together," the conventional subject prepares the reader for the pathos that follows:

If we are separated I will
try to wait for you
on your side of things

your side of the wall and the water
and of the light moving at its own speed
even on leaves that we have seen
I will wait on one side

while a side is there (lines 1-8)

The present tense is a precarious place to be. Loss and absence impinge on all sides. The speaker will wait for the absent you on one side, but only while a side is there. The final line suggests that "a side" could easily vanish, and thus the speaker's waiting would cease. At the same time, one might read the poem's final sentence as an offer to wait forever: walls and water, one could imagine, will always separate this side from that (although unlikely in the eco-poetical world of Merwin's poetry).

As these various examples suggest, absence, as a concept, object, and experience, is a constant subject in Merwin's work. Throughout *The Rain in the Trees* one senses a growing anxiety about the continuation of language as a meaning-making tool. Language is as endangered, one could conclude reading these poems, as any of the endangered flora and fauna the book catalogs. I would like to close with the poem "Native Trees," an elegy of sorts for Merwin's parents:

Neither my father nor my mother knew
the names of the trees
where I was born
what is that
I asked and my
father and mother did not
hear they did not look where I pointed
surfaces of furniture held
the attention of their fingers
and across the room they could watch
walls they had forgotten
where there were no questions
no voices and no shade

Were there trees
where they were children
where I had not been
I asked
were there trees in those places
where my father and my mother were born
and in that time did
my father and my mother see them
and when they said yes it meant
they did not remember

What were they I asked what were they
but both my father and my mother
said they never knew (lines 1-26)

In "Native Trees," the loss is potentially permanent and irremediable. The loss outweighs blame and responsibility. This
loss is one of extinction, a wholly severed connection, and the
effacement of tribal knowledge.

5 The Image

It was the lucidity and legibility of the image that finally led to the dead-end of so many *Imagiste* poems.

: :

Is the image the relic or the reliquary?

: :

In the moment that the image stops the clock, it invents and revives the notion of time.

: :

As much as the image seems a trace of a previous life, it is also a foretaste of an afterlife. Or, at least, the next moment to come.

: :

David Freedberg: "Images work *because* they are consecrated, but at the same time they work *before* they are consecrated. (98)"

: :

The image leaves a mark or trace, which we read as an emanation of the past, that is, as *presence*.

: :

Is the convention of figural arrangement in images of the Annunciation a depiction of decorum or of violence, a seduction or a breaking and entering?

In the image, imbalance suggests movement, a movement to-ward balance and stability.

: :

The image is a lens that deforms time. The image is a lens that deforms space.

: :

Brice Marden: "It's an illusion of an abstraction of things that you see"(35).

: :

Bachelard's notion of the "fabricated image," one without "deep, true, genuine roots," is not what Coleridge might call "fancy," but it is a symptom of what might be called pejoratively "creative writing."

: :

Which is preferable: an image on the point of disappearing, or one too bright to see?

: :

For all its time-worn, subconscious-riddled, elemental and minimalist tendency, the image of the "Deep Image" is really a rather baroque entity, if we see that the baroque vision, as Martin Jay argues, "strives for representation of the unrepresentable and necessarily failing to achieve it, resonates a deep melancholy" (108). Melancholy, enigma, and nostalgia are three coordinates of the "deep image."

: :

The image is the unlocked door between the adjoining rooms of imagination and memory.

: :

The image does not lead to calm, but to disquiet.

: :

Is the image a grave's depth or the mounded dirt that represents the body, the body's displacement of the dirt below?

: :

The image disfigures as it figures.

: :

Ezra Pound's "emotional and intellectual complex in an instant in time(11)" is an apt description of the image, but it fails to note the role of the five senses in our experience of the emotional, the intellectual, and the temporal.

: :

The image is both an experience of and a catalyst for *deja vu*.

: :

The image has been dislodged from its ritual context and thus is weakened.

: :

The image makes an old growth forest out of splinters and sawdust.

: :

The image is not the epitome of the *specific*, of the *detailed*; more often than not it violates more than a few of the Imagist's "A Few Don'ts."

: :

Baudelaire: "The whole of the universe is a store of images and signs to which imagination will give a place and relative value; it is a kind of pasture that the imagination must digest and transform" (49).

: :

The poem is not a system for the reproduction of images, but one for the making of images.

: :

The image is engendered in its rendering.

: :

We remember more the trauma of the image than its imprint, more the suspense of its aftershocks than the surprise of its initial instabilities.

: :

The image does not return you to the world, but to the *gnosis* embodied there.

: :

Thesis: In the image, we see the lightning trace of the maker's hand retreating.
Counter thesis: It is the image's slowness and not its speed that leads at last to the tumbling of the locks.

: :

The poem is both the fever and the dream.

: :

The image allows us to experience time as if it were a landscape.

: :

Through the image, memory forestalls the ephemeral.

: :

The image is rent and thus we can read by the light escaping from its cleft.

6 Variations on the Meditative Mode

In the meditative mode, a poet can undermine the lyric's
drive toward, and love of, closure, without ever giving up
on the moment of lyric insight, what William Wordsworth
calls "spots of time" (line 208), James Joyce calls "epiphanies"
(201), and Virginia Woolf calls "moments of being" (65). Lyric insight within the lyric moment. Since the English Roman-
tics, the clear presence of the pastoral has asserted itself as the
time and space of the meditative utterance much more than as
the bucolic landscape. The mode and method of Wordsworth's
lapsed pastoral, "Lines Composed a Few Miles Above Tintern
Abbey, On Revisiting the Banks of the Wye During a Tour, July
13, 1798," becomes the model for Wallace Stevens' "The Idea of
Order at Key West," a poem that has nothing to do with sheep
or the usual pastoral stage props. Both poems show the vestigial
trace of the eclogue, with Wordsworth turning to and questioning his sister Dorothy, and with Stevens turning to and questioning his companion, Ramon Fernandez. The world before
the poets is a world of their making.

∶ ∶

By staying in the moment, by continuing to turn away from the
lyric's conventions of closure through reflection, refraction,
concentration, continuation, and involution, by troubling the
terms of an argument, by digressing, by spiraling or orbiting
around the lyric moment, pearling the grit of that moment,
one makes mutable the temporality of the meditative space.

∶ ∶

The meditative mode attempts to slow time down, to hold it still, to condense it or stretch it or twist it, without diminishing its vitality or precariousness. The gradations of tense hot-wired into the medium of language allow the *now*, the *then*, and the *to be* to be put under the greatest pressure. The meditative poet is not so much interested in rendering sequential experience, but to attending to the past, the present, and the conditional future as if a trinity embodied as one, as if a single moment, a single point on a plane.

: :

The meditation, as it has come down to us, is an act, the act of the mind upon an object or idea. In the pastoral mode, that object of meditation is often the landscape (and here I distinguish landscape from Nature: the landscape as the land "viewed" and arranged by the reflective and shaping mind). The habits of the meditative mode can be found in the variety of definitions one could give to the verb *to meditate*: to measure, to reflect on, to plan or project the mind, to design in thought, to practice religious or spiritual contemplation, to apply, to continue to apply the mind, to mete out (and if we look up "mete," we discover: to find the quantity, dimension or capacity by rule or standard, to appraise. To define boundaries. To judge).

: :

Alone within the phenomenal world of a landscape and the noumenal world of the in-dwelling mind, the pastoral-meditative poet achieves what Coleridge calls the "grandest efforts of poetry . . . when imagination is called forth, not to produce a distinct form, but a strong working of the mind, still offering what is still repelled, and again creating what is again rejected . . ." (81).

: :

The moment of meditation is, like mythic time, present and ongoing.

7 Variations on Hadrian's Animula

Sun bright, but a thaw hard to imagine. A snow-saddled erratic dominates the clearing. Curves of blue drifts conceal a tumbled stonewall. The brook under ice is tannic with oak leaves. *Why art thou cast down, O my soul? And why art thou disquieted in me?* I *recall* I say, but in truth call after. *After*, belatedly. So much thrown out, trampled under foot. If only words were salt—soluble, savory, vital, electric. Belatedly, I call after. Late spring. The whole sky foxed with stars. The soul: taut, tuned, like a viol—polished, baroque—old fashioned, out of style, a kept keepsake. Crisp with trampled mint, at once preamble and postlude to chance, to change, wind shuffles honeysuckle, exposes a rusted snarl of barbed wire, a rotted post. The soul like a thrown voice, a voice thrown. Clouds pile up all morning for a storm. Or so it seems. *Little soul, errant spark, lost wanderer—O, indweller—you have flown and I grow numb, wan, melancholy, pallid, bereaved, a shell, a shucked husk, emptiness as evidence of your* once-presence. Each new line crossed out. Each old line crossed out. Such satisfaction in the setting down and the crossing out. *O my soul, kin and stranger, wayward guest, waylaid spirit, charm and figment, flame and tear, silvery shiver and cold tremble, belatedly, I call after.* The day begins as always in the dark, then light leaches through, reveals rooftops and walls, an offshore island, its black pines slashed with a gash of gold. How to account for such abundance?

8 An Amnesiac's Meditation on Memory

Memory is the antecedent to dream.

: :

Memory is not an object but the shadow an object casts.

: :

Memory is the magician's empty hands, which suggest the con-cealed they have held all along.

: :

Memory congeals, hardens as amber, around some fragment.

: :

Memory is not immediate but must be worked at—a weight one pulls to the surface like water from a well.

: :

Nostalgia afflicts those with good and bad memories alike.

: :

Memory is not the broken bread, but the falling crust-grit that catches a flash of sunlight.

: :

Burdened by a deep depression, I lost my memory or rather lost my ability to focus the lens to see memory as anything but a blur, a general graininess, a myopic view of distance, an edgeless haze. I had none of the amnesiac's desire, so often dramatized in the soap operas, to piece together a past. Better it remain adrift in the generic, unburden by some looming offstage weather.

: :

How is it the amnesiac always remembers that she has forgotten?

: :

Climb the rungs of memory back to a past? I have only a footstool.

: :

How often the remembered shimmers with the uncanny, like a single glove left behind, turned inside out on the counter.

: :

What did Lazarus remembered, exhumed, dragged back into the light?

: :

I did not lose my memory, but I lost the images by which I recalled memory.

: :

In memory, the cellar is deeper than it ever could have been—irrationally deep—I have to leap from the bottom step into darkness.

: :

The space of memory is emptied. Its volume, its mass gives way to ordinary air, to common water. The scrawl of the cartographer's notes, the reconstructed prairie, the unsealed, unsent letter of ambiguous intent are not forgotten, but gone, erased without a smudge or the paper torn. You can imagine the ease of it: the absenting, the effacement, the names of things, the speed of light, in its transit, superfluous. Without memory there is no desire, or desire is no more than snow on water. Your are fluent at last in the *not knowing*.

: :

I kept my appointment with the devil. He forgot. Stood me up.

9 The Work of Poetry or an Imaginary Plane of Glass Parallel to Sea Level

It takes so little: a ball of twine, a stick, and a box to make a trap; an inkblot on folded paper to render two bears pursued by a dragon, (or is that the moon propped and slumped on twin crutches?); a sharp edge to engrave a mask a dancer might wear to court the rain; The upper quarter of a stone sphere to set a shallow dome above a shallow pit, lit and aglow with the feeble light and dull warmth of an ossuary; a bed of nails on which to rest a sheet of glass.

10 Vestiges

Light elsewhere, I'm sure, but here the bulb's burned out. I breathe wood smoke from a wordless burning bush and am consumed.

: :

Gold (a marriage of sulfur and mercury) cannot escape from gravity's custody. I live in a rice house sealed in sealing wax.

: :

The lotus in Salome's hand shivers in the wind like the torches of an oncoming army. Did we, like the angels, have wings in Eden?

: :

Sleep is a dubious refuge—all flux and instability, a rupture in continuity—and yet I cross over into the underworld and back—only to wake and forget, no wiser.

: :

Nothing in a junkyard is incongruous. At dawn, I re-shelve the moon's slender volume. The cloth-covered bread dough, risen, rises, floats on air.

: :

Biolumenescent lichen are mistaken for wood spirits. The fox's narrow muzzle is damp, matted with blood. So many seas and yet above a single sky.

: :

The bowstring's straight line at a right angle to the wooden curve lets loose an arrow the trajectory of which is a curve.

: :

As Lazarus steps out of the stench and shadows, a dog at Jesus' heel barks, hackles up. The day parcels out its hours one at time.

: :

Every night another entry in the ledger of stars, a bookmark wedged in where tomorrow's counting begins.

: :

Reflection blots transparency. Submerged images seep through. Perhaps wood spirits disguise themselves as lichen.

: :

In the meadow, white birds (or was it *brides*?) Where there is no more time, Augustine argues, there is the fullness of time.

11 Psalm and Lament

In an essay, "On the Purity of Style," Donald Justice writes, "I begin to understand how a critic like [Ivor] Winters can argue that the brief lyric may be greater than a complete tragedy, since the lyric can hope for perfection, an unflawed wholeness and unity" (110). Given that the brief lyric is the dominant mode in Justice's opus, and that as a lyric writer Justice aims for and achieves wholeness and unity, it seems odd that he was ever just beginning to understand Winters' notion. Justice's success as a poet is found in the wholeness and unity of the poems themselves. "I write or try to write as if convinced that, prior to my attempt, there existed a true text, a sort of Platonic Script, which I had been elected to transcribe or record" (138), Justice admits, in "Notes of an Outsider," a series of notebook entries, parables, and aphorisms. In Donald Justice's *Collected Poems*, published in 2004 by Alfred A. Knopf, which collects fifty-six years of poetry, a reader will find "true texts." Justice is a methodical writer, and one might call him, with no pejorative meaning implied, a perfectionist. Word by word, line by line, the poems proceed with subtlety, confidence, modesty, mischief, intelligence, and elegance.

That list of adjectives could be applied to the man as well, who died on August 6, 2004, at the age of seventy-eight. A gifted poet and scholar, Justice was also a painter, composer, and musician, as well as a renowned poker player; an exacting and generous teacher; a supportive friend; and a beloved husband and father who is survived by his wife, the writer Jean Ross, and their son, Nathaniel. Justice's poetry has been honored by grants and fellowships from the Guggenheim Foundation, the Rockefeller Foundation, and the National Endowment for the Arts, and by awards including the Academy of American Poets' Lamont Award, the Pulitzer Prize, and the Bollingen Prize. I first met Justice in 1981, his last year teaching at the Iowa Writers' Workshop before he headed to the University of Florida for a decade. I was starting the MFA program and fortunate enough to have Justice as my first workshop teacher. In my first conference with him, I understood the nature of the apprenticeship he had in mind for me. He read the poem to himself, then read it out loud to me, stumbling where the language faltered. "Hear that," he asked. Yes, I had heard the unfortunate snag and tangle of the line and the sentence. "Hear that," was all he said regarding the words I had on the page. Then he asked that I write five new versions of the poem: one to foreground the narrative, one with the lines shorter—two to three beats—one in which I write about the same subject but without the poem's current language, one in which I change the tense and point of view, and one that was to be either half as long or twice as long. "Can you put them in my office mailbox tomorrow by three o'clock," he asked. More than a little daunted I said, "Yes, sir." Of course, I remember nothing about the poem itself, but I do remember the lesson: that every moment in the poem is an opportunity. My own ear was not tuned finely enough to listen for "Platonic Scripts," but Justice helped me tune my ear for more attentive listening. His comments in conference and in workshop about poetry had a special time-release formula about them, at least for me. That is, I understood them then and there, and found them useful and instructive enough to take me beyond the insight and skill I had at the time. Five years later, I would be working on a poem, or even ten or twenty years later, and think, "Oh, shit, that is what he meant!"

"Mr. Justice is an accomplished writer, whose skill," Howard Nemerov notes in a review of Justice's first book, *Summer Anniversaries* (1960), "is consistently subordinated to an attitude at once serious and unpretentious" (209). Nemerov calls Justice's voice "distinct although quiet" (209). A lazy reader today could easily mistake the quiet and unpretentious for the minor. Justice's first book is published in 1960, placing him in the high drama of the Confessional era, when the quiet and unpretentious might have seemed out of fashion. In 1956, Allen Ginsburg's *Howl* is published. In 1959, W.D. Snodgrass's *Heart's Needle* and Robert Lowell's *Life Studies* follow. Justice's *Summer Anniversaries* is joined in 1960 by Ginsburg's *Kaddish and Other Poems*, Ann Sexton's *To Bedlam and Part Way Back*, and Sylvia Plath's *The Colossus*. The quiet, reticent Justice poems could have easily been drowned out amid the clamor of fraught, psychological voices. Where his contemporaries relied on frankness as one of their experiments, Justice based his experiments in *Summer Anniversaries* upon the most subtle variations and innovation upon conventional and fixed poetic forms.

The weight of the past, and its mutability in memory and in the medium of language, is Justice's primary subject. The past looms real yet uncanny, close at hand yet lost and fallen, palpable yet ghostly. The epigraph to *Summer Anniversaries* announces such a subject:

> O recreate that hour
> Divine Mnemosyne,
> When all things to the eye
> Their early splendor wore (lines 1-4).

Throughout these poems, the elegiac mode dominates, reconciling the past's forfeitures, balancing the past's assets and debts. In this first book, we find a full-grown poet gifted with amazing technical virtuosity, writing sestinas of surprising formal experimentation such as "Here in Katmandu," and "Sestina on Six Words by Weldon Kees," sly variations upon children's rhymes such as "Counting the Mad," a riff on the form of "This Little Piggy," sonnets of extreme emotional intelligence such as "Southern Gothic," and "The Wall." "The Wall," balanced on the fulcrum between the pre- and post-lapsarian world, offers a mythic vision of loss, the tragedy inherent in the retrospective gaze: "They could find no flaw / at all in Eden: This was their first omen (lines 5-6). Like "The Wall," the sestina variation "Here in Katmandu," enacts the conundrum of living in the present tense while facing backward, watching the once-held slip into the distance. The poem boldly abandons the sestina's envoi, leaving the poem lean and knife-sharp. The sestina, through its obsessive form, embodies the very knot of desire it explores: whatever one has, one longs for something else; wherever one is, one longs for elsewhere:

> We climbed the mountain.
> There's nothing more to do.
> It is terrible to come down
> To the valley
> Where, amidst flowers,
> One thinks of snow,
>
> As formerly, amidst snow,
> Climbing the mountain,
> One thought of flowers,
> Tremulous, ruddy with dew,
> In the valley,
> One caught their scent coming down (lines 6-12).

On the mountain, our desire is for the valley; amid snow we long for flowers. Lost things, things beyond our grasp, are still under the influence of our desire's magnetic field:

> It might be possible to live in the valley,
> to bury oneself among flowers,
> If one could forget the mountain,
> How, never once looking down,
> Stiff, blinded with snow,
> One knew what to do.
>
> Meanwhile it is not easy here in Katmandu,
> Especially when to the valley
> That wind which means snow
> Elsewhere, but here means flowers,
> Comes down,
> As so it must, from the mountain (25-36).

In our current period style of poetry where the fragment, blank space, stutter, and stammer are frequent methods of proceeding, where there is little faith in the medium of language it-self to do the work of poetry, where narrative, meditative, and lyric modes are approached with suspicion, to claim Donald Justice as one of the more interesting experimental poets of the last half of the twentieth century may seem more than a little strange, off-kilter, and willingly contrary. From the start, critics praised Justice for the clarity of his voice, the precision of his forms, what Joel O. Connaroe calls Justice's "technical excellence and unpretentious insights(228) ." But Justice, who Anthony Hecht called "the supreme heir of Wallace Stevens" (283), knows well Stevens' adage: "All poetry is experimental poetry" (187). Justice writes in his prose book *Oblivion*:

> I am one of those who like poetry that is difficult, up to a point. It engages more of the whole man; I am bound to it by more ties of association. One is encouraged to go on trying to get beyond the difficulties by a kind of confidence the poem arouses, probably because it looks carefully put together; or it looks brilliant and flashy; or it reminds one of admired passages and thus through re-semblance borrows some authority of previous work. I want to give the name benign obscurity to this kind of difficulty, for there are plenty other kinds which do not work this way, but only leave one feeling rather lost and helpless.... Though sometimes mistaken for it, obscurity is not the path to the sublime; but then in fairness you must add that neither does it defeat the sublime (82).

So where, you might ask, is the experimental difficulty, even the benign obscurity in Justice's poems, which Greg Simon describes as "perfectly flawless poems, moving as inexorably as glaciers toward beautiful comprehension and immersion in reality" (249). T.S. Eliot, discussing difficulty, suggests the poet, "should become more and more comprehensive, more allusive, more indirect, in order to force, to dislocate if nec-essary, language into his meaning" (59). But these are not Jus-tice's methods, whose poems one finds to be particular, direct, and unforced. Justice's poems if they are ever flashy are mod-estly so, and perhaps one of their great difficulties is such modesty. In their minimalism, they make the most of limited and spare elements.

In his next two books, *Night Light* (1967) and *Departures* (1973), Justice experiments with the possibility of newly invented forms, with operations of chance, and with forms that have not borne as much traffic as the sonnet or the sestina. In a tautly wrought poem, "The Thin Man," Justice not only addresses the subject of modesty and self-effacement, but the edginess and threat to those who behold a person bearing such traits. The poem is in five-syllable lines. The form works first and foremost as an obstacle for the writer. The form, as an ornament for the reader, reveals itself slowly and quietly:

> I indulge myself
> In rich refusals.
> Nothing suffices.
>
> I hone myself to
> This edge. Asleep, I
> Am a horizon (lines 1-6).

Throughout *Night Light*, a similar figure appears: a loner, a missing person, a person who wears, as he writes in "The Missing Person," "this last disguise, himself." In "The Tourist from Syracuse," another syllabic poem, Justice reveals the self as one who:

> . . . speaks seldom, and always
> In a murmur as quiet
> As that of crowds which surround
> The victims of accidents.
>
> Shall I confess who I am?
> My name is all names and none.
> I am the used-car salesman,
> The tourist from Syracuse,
>
> The hired assassin, waiting.
> I will stand here forever
> Like one who has missed his bus—
> Familiar, anonymous — (line 14-25)

While Justice may not reject the Eliotic notion of impersonality as much as his Confessional peers, the impersonality he represents is wholly American. In "Men at Forty," Justice presents an aloofness and aloneness one finds in "The Tourist from Syracuse" hybridized with a Wallace Stevens-esque melancholic introspection and a post-World War II suburban tedium:

> They are more fathers than sons themselves now.
> Something is filling them, something
>
> That is like the twilight sound
> Of crickets, immense,
> Filling the woods at the foot of the slope
> Behind their mortgaged houses (lines 15-20.

If "something is filling them," something is lost as well, and that calm, cool absence, whether it be a lapsed Eden or the untroubled hours of childhood, remains, lodged like a splinter.

Justice's insistence on the calm and the cool amplifies the potential threat lurking in the ordinary, the threat that one day will be like the next, as in Stevens' anti-paradise where ripe fruit never falls. In *Departures*, perhaps Justice's most varied, daring, and uneven book, we find even more elaborate formal experimentation and an opening up of subject matter. While the title suggests a move away from where he has been, the poems act more like a new lens with which to see afresh all that he thought he knew. He interrogates his Southern longing for decorum, knowing full well that the grotesque and perverse wait beneath the grammar of manners. Jerome J. McGann argues that "Many of his best poems emerge as nostalgic interior landscapes—empty, silent, and moving to a slow-motion clock," calling this the "silences of the Sphinx, the analyst's reticence, the priest's reserve. Indifference is the appearance of a poetry that is both practical and morally unnerving" (245).

In "Poem," the speaker's unnerving indifference to his reader is offered with candor and the slyest of humor:

> Your type of beauty has no place here.
> Night is the sky over this poem.

It is too black for stars.
And do not look for any illuminations.

You neither can nor should understand what it means.
Listen, it comes without guitar,
Neither in rags nor any purple fashion.
And there is nothing to comfort you.

Close your eyes, yawn. It will be over soon.
You will forget the poem, but not before
It has forgotten you. And it does not matter.
It has been most beautiful in its erasures. (line 13-24)

In the same collection, the wry postmodern voice is coun-
tered by the political in "The Assassinations," by the surreal in
"White Notes," by the riddling in "Things," and by the imita-
tive in "Variations on a Text by Vallejo." Many of Justice's most
anthologized works can be found in *Departures*, which works
more as a miscellany than his next full-length collection, *The
Sunset Maker* (1987), which is a highly unified volume exploring
the Florida of Justice's childhood.

In a new poem from his *Selected Poems* (1979), Justice
foretells the subject and method of *The Sunset Maker*. The poem
is called "Childhood," and it catalogs the peculiar and the particular of 1930s Miami and its "forlorn suburbs." In its original version, the poem was printed with marginalia, explicat-
ing things both ordinary and strange—the Katzenjammer kids,
for instance, or the forthcoming war in Europe. The poem ra-
diates with the historical, the intimate, and the force released
at their collision. "Childhood" concludes with a dedication "to
the poets of a mythical childhood: Wordsworth, Rimbaud, Ril-
ke, Hart Crane, Alberti." In *The Sunset Maker*, we find a poet, to
compare him to the English-speaking poets in the dedication,
Crane-like in his mannerist's figuration and exuberance and
Wordsworthian in his plain spoken voice and in his recollec-
tion and tranquility.

The collection's first poem, "Lines for the New Year,"
announces time and its passage as the fundamental subject of
art and of life:

The old year slips past
      unseen, the way a snake goes.
Vanishes,
        and the grass closes behind it (lines 1-4).

Through memory and imagination, the past and time is pass-
ing, as they do in "My South," sublimely into the mythic:

> . . . the old dream of being a changeling returned.
> The owl cried, and I felt myself like the owl—alone,
>   proud,
> Almost invisible—or like some hero in Homer
> Protected by a cloud let down by the gods to save him.
>   (lines 39-43)

The disinterred past reveals delights in coincidences that can
only be noticed in retrospect. In "Mrs. Snow," a sonnet about
a piano teacher from his childhood, the delight is amplified by
the coincidence of rhyme:

> Busts of the great composers glimmered in niches,
> Pale stars. Poor Mrs Snow, who could forget her,
> Calling the time out in that hushed falsetto?
> (How early we begin to grasp what kitsch is!)(lines 1-4)

Of course, the passage of time is costly and painful, as the
reader finds it in "Psalm and Lament," an elegy for the poet's
mother, "Sometimes a sad moon comes and waters the roof
tiles. / But the years are gone. There are no more years" (lines
25-26). While much of *The Sunset Maker* investigates sentiments,
nostalgias, and a "despair," as Justice writes in "Tremayne,"
"that seems so mild" (line 15), the poet can offer the reader the
burden of boredom and the crumbling edges of despair. The
chilling villanelle, "In Memory of the Unknown Poet, Robert Boardman Vaughn," offers a stark portrait of a friend, a
self-destructive poet:

> It was his story. It would always be his story.
> It followed him; it overtook him finally—
> The boredom, and the horror, and the glory.

Probably in the end he was not sorry,
Even as the boots were brutalizing him in the alley.
It was his story. It would always be his story (lines 1-6).

The exhausting surrender of Robert Boardman Vaughn is memorialized. Justice uses the villanelle's repetitions to hammer down the irreparable and unfortunate fate of the "unknown poet."

Lately he wandered between St. Mark's Place and the
    Bowery,
Already half a spirit, mumbling, and muttering sadly.
O the boredom, and the horror, and the glory (lines 13-
    15).

I have every confidence that Justice, a poet often referred to as a poet's poet, will continue to be read, and not just by poets. Justice's wisdom has been passed along through the oral tradition that is the writers' workshop. His former students include, to mention only a few, Marvin Bell, Rita Dove, Lynn Emanuel, Jorie Graham, Debora Greger, Andrew Hudgins, Mark Jarman, Larry Levis, William Logan, Claire Rossini, Mark Strand, James Tate, and Charles Wright. While his poems offer a thousand and one lessons on the art of poetry, they also offer authentic sentiment and sensation, which the reader experiences as true to experience. The emotion of each poem is balanced to the scale of its language and is never overblown or underfelt. I can only imagine that Justice's posthumous reputation will grow as did the reputation of Elizabeth Bishop, another poet of amazing formal dexterity, whose poems at first seem unassuming, modest, and quiet in spite of their vivid elegance and brilliance.

12 Object Permanence

There are moments in meditation when the world vanishes, and I think in astonishment (attending as I should not) *The world vanished!* Then around me all the space and time fills back in.

: :

Just like that a lake disappears into a sinkhole.

: :

I enter the woods preparing to get lost, go left where I usually go right, uphill where down seems sensible, only to end up back at the creek, to find a fox, midstream, its tail underwater, point with its nose the way home.

: :

It is easy to make the child laugh given the delight she takes in my impermanence.

13 Four Short Essays

At the next table, the waiter quickly and clumsily, with some theatricality, debones with a spoon and knife a branzino (an ocean-going sea-bass that sometimes enters brackish and fresh waters), and presents, with a smile on his face, a plate of tattered and torn flesh to the astonished diner, who says nothing.

: :

The mountain, which measures time by the retreat and advance of glaciers, eclipses from our view the far valley's meadow disheveled by thaw.

: :

Trying to give stern and honest advice to a student, he quotes John Cage, quoting Max Jacob: *Standing in line gives one the opportunity to practice patience*. To which the student replies, "But what can I do to *fix* the poem *now*?"

: :

In a box of old slides from his wife's early travels, he comes across one of his wife nude. Not his wife, but rather the woman he would later meet and marry. In the slide, she is nineteen or twenty, in the woods, her back toward the camera as she looks over her shoulder. He does not know this woman, he realizes, but knows well that look in her eye, even as it does not reflect him.

14 *Ars Poetica*

The edge-land, an emptied scruffy space, gullied and flensed by erosion, ends cliff-side. Sometimes I feel a dis-ease as if a shadow cast its object, as if I had prepared for an accident with inscrutable intent. Below: a ragged coastline, snarls of contorted bladderwrack. As the tide turns a shingled spit emerges. I never wish to jump, but to step out onto air, where sea and fog and sky are a single element. It almost seems possible to stay aloft.

15 *Duende* and Gravity

When I think about *duende*, I think of the poet Larry Levis, because it was from Levis that I first heard of *duende*. Philip Levine was in town and had given a reading. Levis and his wife, the poet Marcia Southwick, hosted a reception at their home after the reading. As the party thinned out, I hung on (I was an undergraduate. There was free food and booze) and I joined into a circle of folks—Levis, Levine, Southwick, and a couple of grad students talking about *duende* and playing a sort of parlor game: *Duende—Who's Got It*? Miles Davis or Stan Getz? Janis Joplin or Joni Mitchell? And when the circle came around to me, Larry asked: Neil Young or Mick Jagger? I said Neil Young and they all moaned NO! Larry said, "You can't sing about a house in North Ontario and have *duende*."

: :

Lorca writes, "Duende is a force not a labor, a struggle not a thought. I heard an old maestro of the guitar say: 'The duende is not in the throat: the duende surges up, inside, from the soles of the feet.' Meaning, it's not a question of skill, but of a style that's truly alive: meaning, it's in the veins: meaning, it's of the most ancient culture of immediate creation" (49).

So *duende* is not inherent in the performer, but in the given performance. I was too shy that night at the reception to debate, but if I had defended my choice I might have said something like this: So, Mick Jaggar might possess *duende* as he sings "Give Me Shelter" or "Tumbling Dice," but does not, I am sure, on a recording from my high school days, "Fool to Cry," a syrupy ballad: "Ooo Oooo, Daddy you're a fool to cry.

. ." The sentimental song, with a whiny falsetto, went on forever. It is rumored in fact that Keith Richards fell asleep on stage in Germany once performing the song.

At that same moment in history, Neil Young had a song called "The Revolution Blues," a sort of Charles Mason-esque persona poem: "I hear that Laurel Canyon is full of famous stars./ I hate them worse than lepers and I kill them in their cars." But aside from the gory lyrics, what gives the song gravity is the guest rhythm section of Rick Danko on what can only be describe as a lead bass guitar and Levon Helm on drums, the two playing as they never did behind Dylan in The Band. So, Young's Canadian pastoral of "Helpless" as a performance may have no *duende*, but "The Revolution Blues" with the iron-edged feedback of Young's guitar and the driving rhythm of Danko and Helm just might weigh in as *duende*.

: :

"Two forces," Simone Weil says, "rule the universe: light and gravity" (1). Of these two forces, *duende* is most influenced by gravity. Lorca writes: "This 'mysterious force that everyone feels and no philosopher has explained' is, in sum, the spirit of the earth." We connect to it where gravity holds us to the earth: "the *duende*," remember, "surges up, inside, from the soles of the feet" (49). Most of the examples Lorca cites in his talk of duende are from music and dance—Flamenco, in particular. "Every art and every country," Lorca assures us, "is capable of *duende*" (55).

: :

Now out at the edge of the solar system, the Voyager spacecrafts are almost beyond the reach of the sun's gravity. Launched in 1977, a couple of years after the Stone's recorded "Fool to Cry," and still a year before their best-selling album "Some Girls," is released, one of the Voyager spacecrafts carries a golden record that contains a wide variety of music to represent humanity to whatever alien civilization might find the craft and have a record player handy. The music includes Bach, Beethoven, an Indian raga, Peruvian panpipes, Chuck Berry's "Johnny B. Goode," and many works of world music. I want to think about one song on that golden record in particular, Blind Willie Johnson's "Dark was the Night." If America has a folk music tradition similar to Flamenco it is the blues, which shares west and north African roots.

This blues song takes its title from the lyrics of an eighteenth-century hymn "Gethsemane": "dark was the night and cold was the ground / on which my Lord was laid." So, we locate ourselves pre-crucifixion: Jesus awaits capture, torture, and execution, awake in the garden while his followers sleep, awake in the dark night of the soul. Beneath the length of his body is the cold earth, the tug of gravity and the grave. Above him, the dark night weighs down. The image is paralleled a few scenes down the road, when Jesus is lowered from the cross and set down on the cold ground, a dead man—the story, it seems over, seemingly beyond miracle.

Johnson's song is a wordless song, a haunting, wiry slide guitar played with a penknife and not a bottleneck, his low mournful voice moaning, shaping no words, his voice and the whine of the slide at times inseparable in their lamentation. The aliens, listening to this forlorn, almost ambient music will begin to imagine the felt depth that is *duende*—no—will be embodied by it and, like Blind Willie Johnson, will not need words to shape it.

To think of the plaintive cries and heartbroken humming of Blind Willie Johnson being played beyond the edges of the solar system is, for me, an almost sublime thought. And as I think of the sublime, I think how *duende* is, in fact, the opposite of the sublime. Rather than feeling minute beneath the immense weight of all that looms above us as in the sublime, in the experience of *duende* we find within ourselves an endless depth as large as a universe. Like the sublime, *duende* is the experience of awe at the scale of the human in relation to the universe: the awe of awesomeness and the awe of awfulness.

: :

Larry Levis and Marcia Southwick left Columbia, Missouri the following year to teach at the Iowa Writers Workshop. In Iowa City, Larry began composing what is my favorite book of his, *Winter Stars*, a book I think of as his mythic autobiography, which begins with recollections of childhood, then moves on to the death of his father and the disintegration of his marriage and his mourning of both losses. We follow him, in the long expansive poems at the end into a kind of exile that is as much located in grief as it is upon a map. Many of these poems possess *duende*, in particular a poem called "The Cry," about a descent into the gravity of darkness. The poet possesses *duende*, guided more by a kind of self-destructive demon than by a muse or an angel.

The first half of the poem hovers in the realm of what Coleridge would call "the fancy." Things seem somewhat made-up rather than made *from* experience: "the smalltime-business men . . . smelling of pomade" (line 15), and "the town's one gambler" (line 17). But even in the opening we get peculiar and particular details that ring harrowingly true: "the aging Palomino slept/ Standing up in the moonlight, with one rear hoof slightly cocked.(lines 5-6)" Then in the second half, beginning with "On my last night as a child, that sleep was final" (line 29), the weight and pull of *duende* gathers and amasses. The speaker sees "every detail that disappointment had sketched (line 42)" on the exposed nude bodies of his aging parents, sees it and embodies it so convincingly as:

> The stooped shoulders & sunken chest of my father,
> Sullen as the shape of a hawk in wet weather,
> The same shape it takes in its death,
> When you hold it in your outstretched hand,
> And wonder how it can shrink to so small a thing.
>   (lines 47-52).

I experience *duende* with the poet as a "force not a labor, a struggle not a thought" (49).

16 On the Occasion of the Release of the Senate Torture Report

In Piero della Francesca's "Flagellation of Christ," the room is needlessly spacious for the blunt work at hand. Three figures in the foreground take no notice of the violence. Except for the purpose of composition, they are superfluous. Some critics argue these three are Nicodemus, Joseph of Arimathea, and the beloved disciple John, who will later bribe the authorities, claim the body of their friend, and bury him in a borrowed grave once the humiliations, beatings, and execution end. At this distance, Jesus appears to console his tormenter, whose right hand is raised (one can barely see the whip) as if in protest. Who has not been like this man who beats another man and feels put upon?

17 The Form of a Walk

"Poetry," Robert Frost argues, "begins in reading books," and the poet "writes out of the eddy in his mind of all the books he ever read . . . . The whole thing is performance and prowess and feats of association" (3). Anyone reading my first two books, published in the 1980s, would see the connection to Frost, but in all honesty, I had read very little Frost at the time, except for the anthology pieces. If I *knew* Frost, I knew him secondhand by way of the influence he had on poets I found myself reading in the late 1970s and the early 1980s: Seamus Heaney, Philip Levine, Elizabeth Bishop, and James Wright, to name a few.

Nonetheless, the publicity people at Atheneum drafted jacket copy for my second book that read, very much to my surprise: "Eric Pankey is a poet of weather and seasons, and he deals with them with easy authority, not unlike a young Robert Frost." We won't trouble here just what that blurb-ese means: "easy authority," "not unlike." But that comparison demanded that I dig deep into Frost's work, become intimate with what I had only known as a kind of hand-me-down influence.

Much of the teaching I have done over the last quarter-century has focused on the nature of, the habits of, and the possibilities of the lyric poem in the twentieth and twenty-first centuries. I have written elsewhere about the tendencies of the lyric poem: its singular purpose; its efficiency; its rush toward closure; its close and enclosing orbit around the moment of a thing perceived, a thing felt, a thing understood, if only momentarily. I have written as well about a lyric sub-genre, the meditation or the meditative poem (of which Frost is a master) where the poet stays "in" the lyric moment, by continually turning away from the conventions of closure by way of reflection, refraction, concentration, continuation, and involution, by troubling the logic of narrative, the terms of an argument; by digressing; by spiraling around; or by pearling the grit at the heart of that lyric moment.

Today, I would like to think about a kind of meditative *form* that is as well a meditative *subject*: the walk. Many of my favorite poems take the form of a walk. Two of my earliest favorites are William Wordsworth's "Lines Compose a Few Miles Above Tintern Abbey," and Wallace Stevens's "Idea of Order at Key West." In these two poems, we find out late in the game that our walkers are not solitary but have, in fact, been accompanied on their walks: Wordsworth by his sister Dorothy and Stevens by one Ramon Fernandez. I began to look for poems the shape of which and the subject of which were walks, in particular, solitary walks, poems like Gary Snyder's "A Walk," or A. R. Ammons's "Corson's Inlet," which concludes beautifully:

> that there is no finality of vision,
> that I have perceived nothing completely,
> that tomorrow a new walk is a new walk(151).

Let me be clear, a walk, the sort of walk I am talking about, is not a hike. A walk is not a trip, not a planned journey. It begins without a destination in mind and unfolds, unravels before you. The walk like the poem is not seeking as Ammons' suggests "finality" or "completion," but an attentive-ness and perhaps even a distracted-ness within the moment of moving and perceiving.

Let us consider Robert Frost's "The Wood-pile." The speaker of our poem is on a walk, a common enough journey, and one without a premeditated destination. In fact, he walks where, in three other seasons, he might not: in a swamp, which is by its nature unwelcoming: soft underfoot, boggy, buggy, pathless, all rank and welter. . . .

Now winter, the slime and muck, "a frozen swamp" (line 1), can hold him up, and thus he can venture in. Yet, only a line into the poem our speaker gives up on entering inward.

He "pauses," stating first: "I will turn back from here. (line 2)" And having interrupted his journey, he changes his mind about changing his course, and says "No, I will go on farther— and we shall see" (line 3). That first-person plural invites us along on the walk and we wonder what exactly it is we shall see. "We shall see" (line 3). Is that even a statement about the sights ahead or is it an admission of uncertainty that we might translate as "Who knows?"

The walk, thus far, merely three lines into the poem, is one of hesitations, qualifications, stops and starts, and it continues in such a fashion. Things are stable, then they are not: "The hard snow held me, save where now and then/ One foot went through. (line 4-5)" The particulars of the place do not distinguish it, but, in fact, make it indistinguishable:

> The view was all in lines
> Straight up and down of tall slim trees
> Too much alike to mark or name a place by
> So as to say for certain I was here
> Or somewhere else (lines 5-9)

All the speaker can say for sure is that he is "far from home" (line 9), where one assumed the snow and ice holds one up, where the trees are distinct enough to be landmarks so that one know where one is.

Is he lost? Or does he just not know where he is? Are these the same thing or different experiences? Why should we care to follow such a hapless guide into such unpromising territory? Then a bird appears:

> A small bird flew before me. He was careful
> To put a tree between us when he lighted,
> And say no word to tell me who he was
> Who was so foolish as to think what *he* thought.
> He thought that I was after him for a feather—
> The white one in his tail; like one who takes
> Everything said as personal to himself.
> One flight out sideways would have undeceived him.
>   (lines 10-17)

The description of the bird seems in many ways a mirror of our speaker, an act of self-portraiture, who seems to take everything he experiences "as personal to himself": the snow will not hold him up, the trees will not guide his way, the bird—did he expect it to?—will say no word to him.

How much ground has been covered during this little delirious reverie about the bird?

If a walk is taken without a thought of an end point, then our speaker's digression about the bird is not unlike his other stops and starts so far in the poem. The subject of the poem has been and continues to be what comes into view next. If our speaker is uncertain of his location, the bird perhaps has taken on the role of guide and scout. Or perhaps the bird has led him astray. The speaker continues:

> And then there was a pile of wood for which
> I forgot him and let his little fear
> Carry him off the way I might have gone (18-20),

"The way I might have gone," confirms that the walker's intent was to keep walking, but the double conjunction of "And then," announces we have arrived at the effect of all the previous causes, hesitations, and detours thus far in the poem:

> It was a cord of maple, cut and split
> And piled—and measured, four by four by eight.
> And not another like it could I see.
> No runner tracks in this year's snow looped near it.
> And it was older sure than this year's cutting,
> Or even last year's or the year's before.
> The wood was gray and the bark warping off it
> And the pile somewhat sunken. Clematis
> Had wound strings round and round it like a bundle.
> What held it though on one side was a tree
> Still growing, and on one a stake and prop,
> These latter about to fall (23-33).

The wood-pile stands in the midst of a swamp—cut, split, stacked, built by another's hand, another who had ventured as our speaker has into this unwelcoming and impractical place. This wood-pile, upon which much labor has been spent to gather and arrange, is left to the will of entropy. It has begun to sink into the soft earth of the swamp, the clematis has wrapped and bundled it and would in another season camouflage it. Our speaker might not have even noticed it in full summer. The handy-work that shored up the pile is about to give way to ruin.

And as he turns his thoughts to an absent other, this maker of a seemingly useless thing, one senses the speaker continues his act of self-portraiture—is not the making of a poem a similar labor on which one spends oneself, imagining while writing that the labor *is* practical, that the poem might be of *some* use, but in the end, the finished poem is left behind as the poet pursues new tasks, new poems. The poem is left behind for others to stumble upon.

> I thought that only
> Someone who lived in turning to fresh tasks
> Could so forget his handiwork on which
> He spent himself, the labor of his ax,
> And leave it there far from a useful fireplace
> To warm the frozen swamp as best it could
> With the slow smokeless burning of decay(lines 34-40).

The last two lines of this poem have been much discussed elsewhere and are to my mind flawless, so I would like to let them stand beyond paraphrase.

18 Ideal Proportions

Nothing remains of the ladder but a splintered rung.

: :

As per the terms of the surrender the road is paved with the ash of the fallen.

: :

In the cave of a thousand enlightenments, a diagram of the distance between stars.

: :

A map of the underworld on the wing of a cicada.

: :

Even broken the vessel possessed ideal proportions.

: :

The spectrum is calibrated from transparency to opacity.

: :

A ship cast forth despite the forecast, the ship that founders now in the offing.

19 Among Thorns: Drafts and Fragments

Wallace Stevens's "Last Look at Lilacs" resembles the bitterness of missed sexual opportunity found in his uncollected poems "Red Loves Kit," "Good Man, Bad Woman," and "The Woman Who Blamed Life on a Spaniard": "What is it/That marries her innocence thus" (Lines 7-8). Certainly not the unnamed *I* who holds her in his specular gaze. His *holding* and *not holding* is what riles him, is what provokes his self-hatred. Perturbed by lust and admonished by unrequited desire, he sees himself as pathetic, bathetic in his *maleness*, and must invent a "Don John" who will embrace her, who in rugged arrogance *takes* what the I/eye can only gaze upon in an appropriating manner. One sees this also in "From the Misery of Don Joost": the woman *as* reflection will not offer the gazer the reflection he believes he *should* behold.

: :

Matter and the Spirit: the *material world* as *dark matter* that the divine cannot see and thus not attend.

: :

Fugue—Latin: *fuga*, flight—each voice is fleeing the one that comes after it.

: :

In the lyric, language is both the ritual and the sacrifice at the moment's altar.

To wait is to be in the midst of things, to not yet have arrived. To wait is to be full of anticipation. To wait is to be full of tedium. To wait is, at times, to experience both of these at once. Certainly, ritual and prayer are a kind of enactment, a kind of communication that attempts to interrupt that static, the stasis, to break through the mundane and perhaps access the sacred. Such mystical experiences are rare, or are, at least, rare in my experience.

The business of a lyric poet is to be attentive, attentive to the medium of poetry and attentive to the world. Sometimes the lyric poet uses the medium to make of the moment something momentous. Sometimes the lyric poet uses the medium to capture what is barely there: the fleeting, the ephemeral, a peripheral glimpse. On either side of the moment there is waiting.

: :

It is not resemblance that compels, but difference we are asked to see as resemblance that evokes mystery.

: :

The poem is not a vessel for thought, not a receptacle for what the poet has previously known. The poem is a way of thinking, a vehicle for that thinking, a way of writing toward what one does not know.

: :

The imagination is a hooded falcon.

: :

The homeless body of the dead Jesus is filed away in a borrowed grave. The unresolvable nature of guilt and grace is unbearable.

: :

Enigma=Melancholy

The poem begins in disequilibrium. One must enter into, or remove oneself from, the chaos in order to see its order.

: :

All one summer I hung sheet rock, breathed gypsum, moved as a worn-out ghost of sweat and chalk bound to gravity. When I snapped a plumb line, the ideal, however temporary, left its mark: blue, deft, spare, and of course, easily smudged. My days were a calibration of work and sleep, folding money I had no time to spend or waste. And now that the plumb line is gone, the particulars blur: days maroon in the general, days like other days, a passage one has crossed like a dream and forgets. Forty years ago, I knew the precise weight of the hammer, the taste of the nail on my tongue, but now that whole summer is a day at most, eight hours of hard work, hardly worth remembering.

: :

Writing: little pleasure these days. Like a sore spot in my gums and digging at it with a toothpick.

: :

With *The Southern Cross*, *The Other Side of the River*, and *Zone Journals*, Charles Wright's meditations have become more and more inclusive, allowing lush lyricism, confident statement, straight-forward narrative, the distances of history, and a geography as large as the imagination to work within a single poem toward the argument of its particular idea. These poems are full of so much information that, upon first reading, it is hard to believe that a structure could hold and sustain such difficult and various content. The shape of the poems is loose, the lines pushing out toward the right-hand side of the page, stair-stepping downward. Wright's poems are rich in their intricacy. Their difficulty is not in their expansiveness, but in their absolute clarity. Wright charges each line with an equal energy; each shines as brightly as the next. What keeps his poems from being merely poetic, a blinding light of beautiful language, is how the line of thought continually asserts itself, how the mind is at once complex and inclusive as it distills intellectual, carnal, and spiritual experience. Memory and history, the image and the rhetoric, the questions and the answers, the diurnal and the sublime are all equal integers in the poems' long equations. If Wright's meditation's are like essays, they leave out all transition, all connective material, all the normal gear-shifting of logic. We might be tempted, if the poems were not so well-wrought line by line, to read them as poems of process.

: :

In the lyric poem: Tone>Narrative

: :

Form is a confrontation with a given language's limitations.

: :

The Early Education of the Poet

My sixth-grade teacher accused me of plagiarism on an in-class writing assignment she had us do one day in about fifteen minutes before recess, which made me think, "This must be good if she thinks a grown-up wrote it." So, I became curious about poems, what a real poem might sound like. This led me to the public library where I began to read all the collections of poetry I could find—Eliot, Roethke, Moore, H.D., Donne, Wilbur, Hopkins, Stevens—not judging, not really understanding all that much, but enthralled by the spell of the words. Of course, at the same time, I loved popular music, and lyrics were another way into understanding the effect of many poetic conventions, particularly the possibility of the echo of sounds in a line and how images can haunt. I can recall being amazed by lines by Bob Dylan such as, "The ghost of electricity howls in the bones of her face" ("Visions of Johanna), or "When you're lost in the rain in Juarez and its Eastertime too" ("Just Like

Tom Thumb's Blues"), or "The wind howls like a hammer / The night blows cold and rainy / My love she's like some raven / At my window with a broken wing" ("Love Minus Zero/No Limit"). So from seventh grade on, I was a regular reader of poetry, and once I reached high school I had a handful of excellent teachers who lead me to other poets, to poetry readings, to literary journals. They took me seriously enough that I began to take myself seriously, and they encouraged me to send out work to journals. Some things were taken and, responding well to positive reinforcement, I have kept on sending out.

: :

The pattern on the rug is of a paradise, an abstraction that welcomes and excludes, as wall after wall encloses an oasis.

: :

Some Kinds of Poets

(A riff on some concepts from an art exhibit on melancholy and painting I half-remember from a 1994 visit to Venice.)

—one who desires to preserve and conserve without transformative logic.
—one who is a collector, obsessively iterating the object.
—one who finds it impossible to intervene in the world's transformations, exacerbating one's role as a privileged but impotent observer.
—one whose mind opens in circles of segregations, ruins, and repetitive patterns, incessantly building to destroy, to rebuild. . . .

: :

One problem with Surrealism: the tendency to make the erotic and the profane tedious.

: :

Like the alchemist, the poet wrestles with ordinary materials, puts pressure and heat upon them toward transmutation.

: :

The poem: the *of* in *object of desire.*

: :

In his essay, "'Ulysses,' Order and Myth," T. S. Eliot describes a way of writing he calls "the mythic method," which, he claims, manipulates "a continuous parallel" between contemporary moments and moments in antiquity, "a continuous parallel (175)" between what one experiences in the here and now and what one experiences as the ongoing *now-ness* of the ancient and the mythic. A reading of James George Frazer's *The Golden Bough: A Study in Magic and Religion,* informs much of Eliot's thinking in this essay about James Joyce's *Ulysses* and informs Eliot's composition of his own long poem, *The Waste Land.* The strength of *The Golden Bough,* a breakthrough work of comparative oral and folk narratives, is, as scholar Robert Fraser puts it "that, as pages unfurl, each of its readers out of his very individual experience, evinces the distinct impression that he is remembering something" (193). In *Associationism and the Literary Imagination,* Cairns Craig writes,

> What *The Golden Bough* provided for its readers was a model of the human mind bound together by associations rooted in prehistory, and a demonstration of how the fragmentary remains of ancient rites and myths could be reconstructed by retracing their (possible) associative interconnections. And what it suggested, was the power of those ancient associations—the 'engrams' of prehistory—to resist the progressive development of civilization: on the *tabula* of the mind later writing does not obscure or obliterate earlier texts—rather, it is the later writing that fades rapidly to leave only the outlines of almost forgotten script. (193)

For creative writers, the study of folklore reminds us of the value of the past, of all the previous tales, ballads, and texts that have preceded us, how each text rises out of contexts—ritual, ceremony, seasonal celebration, familial stories, significant occasions. "Eliot's assessment of the mythic method," Nicolas Andrew Miller, writes in *Modernism, Ireland, and the Erotics of Memory*, "went well beyond the description of a formally innovative technique to link modernism as such specifically to the project of remembering differently. The mythic method, Eliot suggested, consists in a kind of radical affirmation of the past's currency in the imaginative description of present experience" (5). The mythic method is not a modern invention, merely a modern description of the method writers throughout history have used to weave a parallel double helix of past and present into an enigmatic and radiant sense of a thing individually and tribally remembered.

: :

Visionary poetry is a translation of the vision and not a transcription.

: :

The locus of the lyric is a threshold.
        Often in the lyric, the narrative is hidden: the motivation for joy or despair left unsaid and unstaged.

: :

A life of faith requires a stamina gained only by a practice of faith.

: :

As if is the scale on which the unequal is measured.

: :

It is not obscurity, but obliqueness that delights.

A confession in poetry should have little to do with admitting (*testifying* as we said at the tent revival) but with the revelation of what the poet, until now, has not had language to reveal.

: :

My daughter Clare at four years old describing her drawing: *It's a picture of the Holy Spirit. It's invisible so I gave it a face.*

: :

Are the Gospels a story of hospitality or a lack of hospitality?

Nothing makes one's body feel more extrinsic than sickness or sin.

The despair—not the relief—to learn that one is not responsible for everything.

: :

Line=a hybrid unit of interval and tension.

The trick is to tune it finely enough to make something that vibrates with music.

: :

Craft is always the dirty word in discussions of creative writing pedagogy: "All you can teach them is craft." One can certainly attempt to teach craft—something about the history of the language, the history of poetic convention, the practice of poetic conventions—as a way to give young writers power and dexterity. *CRAFT*=ART, CUNNING, POWER. All we can teach are skills to be practiced and we can hope that those skills empower. We cannot provide vision or character. But sometimes and on rare occasion the practice of craft leads a young poet to vision and builds character.

: :

Enigma is latent in the commonplace—latency as the essence of enigma.

: :

Listening to the *Art of the Fugue* late last night played by the Juilliard String Quartet, I realized my various attempts to capture the fugue-like in verse are impossible, for it is after all the coupling and tangling and unknotting and unthreading of more than one voice that equals the fugue. A poem can offer only one voice at a time, and any attempt at multiple voices must offer each voice one at a time. They must line up in single file, say their lines, and make way for the next. The best I can do is through refrain and variation, obsessive repetition. And yet what I long for is the intimate and glorious brooding of Bach's "Contrapunctus 14."

: :

The curve of time appears a straight line for the short span of a life.

: :

We trust the t-square and the dangled bob's chalk mark to tell us what is straight and plumb. We trust the tools we own are worthy of trust, that they are well-calibrated and durable. The rub of the rasp and the scrape of the plane might reveal the grain, might knock off the rough edges, but if the flaw is in the wood itself, what good then is craft or work?

: :

As I reread *The Four Quartets* I keep hearing John Donne's "And makes me end, where I begun." And the joy is not so much my return to Eliot, but to Donne, where he and Eliot are least alike:

> Our two souls therefore, which are one
>   Though I must go, endure not yet
> A breach, but an expansion,
>   Like gold to aery thinness beat. (20-24)

Eliot's power in his long poem is in the large sweep, the accumulation. Here and elsewhere in Donne it is the nudging and, at times, slamming together of two words and the charge they release that brings joy.: breach/expansion, batter/heart, personed/God.

: :

I tell my students that there is no such thing as a "writer's block." There are times when you are writing and times when you are preparing to write. I like to think of all my preparation for writing as the writing itself—reading books, walking the dog, going to movies, having dinner with friends, going to readings. Putting things down on paper is just one aspect of writing.

: :

The narrative urge is to place trust in the moment that comes next. The lyric urge is to hold the present moment still. But the meditative poem attempts to envelop the moment and understand it (intellectually, philosophically, spiritually?) through circumspection and concentration.

: :

It is easier to have faith in the sound of a bit of language—a syllable, a rhyme—than it is to have faith in what I *meant* to say.

: :

What does one do having put the past in order? Can an act in the present dislodge the past from its stasis and transform it? How long was I frozen, besieged by the weight and guilt of past deeds—unable to move or act in the moment of the present?

: :

Through the act of the poem, through the vehicle of the poem, I hope to come closer to that which remains a mystery.

: :

ALLEGORIA SACRA: A little mound of rice on a shallow metal plate is an offering. Its function: *to be set aside.* A ritual is not a habit, but one performs it, occupies and inhabits its time and space. Someone explained imaginary numbers to me more than once. They are hard to imagine, even with the formula, even if imaginary. Easier this plate of rice.

: :

T. S. Eliot's work offers three interesting methods of approaching the sacred in poetry:

1. The prophetic, apocalyptic, and eschatological voice (or voices) in *The Waste Land*, written when he was not a Christian, I know, but when he was using such texts as Luke's Gospel and a good bit of Western, Christian-tinged literature and holy Eastern texts for collage and sampling.

2. The mystical/visionary voice in "Ash Wednesday" and to some degree in "Marina" and "Journey of the Magi," evocative in its mystery, intensity, and in its liturgical echoes.

3. The discursive, meditative voice in *The Four Quartets*, with its ruminations on timelessness, history, *self*, and the lapsed Edenic realm that is memory.

: :

Not a spark, but a splinter of God in each of us, inflamed, working its way to the surface.

: :

Poets must speculate upon the language itself or else they have only memory and its cargo of losses.

: :

The poem is not a *space* one can master, but a *time* one cannot.

: :

One way to consider originality is one's differentiation from the very canon to which one is apprenticed. Another is one's individual translation of that canon. These are just two ways.

: :

Czeslaw Milosz has said the Fall and original sin are for him the key mystery. Throughout his work, the poet recalls the lost garden and that time before consciousness and duality. Adam's task becomes the poet's task, to name and catalog what is and can be known. Such a task is fraught with contradiction. One is given dominion and yet, by naming, one holds in memory and foresees what can be and will be lost. Milosz is both at home and in exile in the world. The memory of the province he once inhabited haunts and enchants him. Although he is autobiographical at times he is rarely confessional. Whatever his sin, original or not, he does not say. He returns to what is lost and to what can be held, kept, or preserved. His pose is that of the chronicler whose one hope is history, time made flesh in memory and language; yet memory and language are each in its way a disappointment to the poet. Where other poets might find solace, Milosz finds durable paradox against which philosophy, theology, and poetry do their limited work.

: :

Let me describe my process. I tend to keep notebooks into which I jot down words, images, lines, as well as the usual sort of notes one keeps when reading or going to museums. My poems usually begin with a return to such notebooks, notebooks from various times and various travels. I flip through and try to find language that interests me, language that snags me in some way. Say something like "tragedy fed on wolf's milk." When I come upon it I cannot usually recall the original context in which I wrote that down, but I am attracted to its strangeness and start looking for a way it might find a life and home in a poem. What is the speech act, what is the lyric moment out of which one might say something like "tragedy fed on wolf's milk?" I feel as if I am rarely writing poems, but in these notebooks I am constantly writing lines and phrases, words I need to look up or to look into their etymology. My poems are in many ways collages of my own writing, and I do spend a good bit of time moving things around so that what might have ended a poem in an earlier draft might now be the starting place. The process is simple—I place images next to each other and see what resonance is set going between them or among them. I am not trying to say something, I am trying to find a way into a language that is strange and disquieting to me.

: :

I step back into depression as I might step into a puddle, only to find myself in over my head.

: :

The dog says, "Like you, I read all the time. Most of it is shit."

: :

Poetry is a speculative mode. The tendency of poetry is wholeness—it dares to speak, to give shape, to attempt wholeness within complexity, when other forces long for division and fragmentation. If politics is the enactment of power—force, violence, control—its language is the language of lie, deception, misinformation, rumor, and the withheld. Politics prefers innuendo. In politics, one admits only to the most recent revision and never to the existence of an earlier draft. Poetry is no match for the political, because the political has its mind made up.

: :

From the start, James Tate has had an ear for phrasing and a sense of timing that leaves a reader off-guard. The reader comes to expect the unexpected. Tate is our Poor Tom, who leads us in each poem to a precarious edge. If we listen, the crazy babbling of the Fool is tuned beyond static to a true and haunting music. Tate's poems convey a stark vision, and yet he refuses the role of visionary, preferring, at every turn, contrariness, the quick change-up, the pie-in-the-face, and the punch line. Even as I laugh, heartily laugh at and with his poems, the laughter is nervous laughter, an uneasy wait for the inevitable pathos and slapstick. The world of Tate's poems is a world of mistakes, mishaps, and miscommunications, and the comedy in that world is antic, manic, clownish, and black. At the end of his comedy, community is not brought back together. The happiest *ever after* offered in his poems is the preservation of the mundane.

: :

Hard to write the poetry of my depression because depression is mute, lethargic, articulate primarily as stalled-ness, stilled-ness, stupor.

: :

Depressed, I am reminded that each thing, each moment ruthlessly *is*.

: :

Student explaining why his poem is called "Untitled": "I wanted to capture the sensation of my inability to think of a title."

: :

I have always liked this little parable by Chuang Tzu: "Long ago, a certain Chuang Tzu dreamt he was a butterfly—a butterfly fluttering here and there on a whim, happy and carefree, knowing nothing of Chuang Tzu. Then all of a sudden he woke to find that he was, beyond all doubt, Chuang Tzu. Who knows if it was Chuang Tzu dreaming a butterfly, or a butterfly dreaming Chuang Tzu (31)?"

　　Lyric poems often have at their heart a moment of metamorphosis, of transformation, of sudden insight, of momentary awareness. And often those moments occur at a place of between-ness—a threshold between one place and another, between one kind of awareness and another. I would say that I am not trying to distinguish these states of consciousness, but to investigate the permeable (if one is lucky) barrier between the two and see what happens when one crosses over and back across that threshold as an epic hero might descend into and climb back up from the underworld. But my purpose is always that of lyric poetry and not that of the epic.

: :

Some see poetry as the enemy of *meaning*. What if that is its virtue and not its vice?

: :

The poem: a setting for a spectacle.
The poem: a rehabilitation of words.
The poem should challenge and not confirm perception.
The poem should transfigure as it figures.
The poem dramatizes vision by way of words: words that in no way *as visual objects* simulated the visualized.
The poem: homage to the ephemeral.
The poem: what the mind did not know: embodied now, suspended in language.

: :

I always imagined that one day my faith would be solid and certain, a kind of bedrock upon which one might build, a sturdy foundation, but ebb and flow has been my experience of faith: something liquid, shifting, mutable, something that, from the proper distance in space and time, might seem stable, but lived minute by minute, day to day, or articulated in poem after poem, shape-shifts before our eyes. There is a phrase in common parlance now that seems apt. One does not believe or *have* faith, but one is on a *faith journey*. Mine has been a journey full of dead-ends and washed-out roads, of elaborate detours and traffic jams, of getting lost and finding myself surprisingly found, of short-cuts, flat tires, and more than a few miles hitchhiking. Along the way, a few lovely overlooks, endless stretches of smooth pavement. In retrospect, I see no other way to have arrived *here*.

ERIC PANKEY

In Charles Wright's poems one finds a flawless ear for the melodic and rhythmic possibilities of the free verse line in the American language. Wright possesses an alchemist's touch with the image and a luminist's eye for the light that reveals and transfigures the given world. The given is what Wright continues to confront and trouble. His habit is that of a pilgrim on a spiritual itinerary, at times open-hearted, at times flint-hearted to the journey and the sojourn. Sadness often reigns over these meditations—an eschatological melancholia imbues them with weight, gravity, and a magnitude of wisdom, delivered, at times, with the wit of truth plainly said. The answers he seeks, he knows, are there *in* the landscape or accessible *through* the landscape, but they are not yet found, not yet revealed. As a result, the meditations open in circles outward, attempting both to preserve what cannot be preserved—the past and the future— and to transcend it. *Gnosis* is the destination of Wright's poems, but the path they offer is by no means spare or ascetic. Few poets can conjure as well made a line as Charles Wright, and even fewer can offer lines that grow more beautiful, more complex, and more true each time we return to them.

: :

Charles Wright writes of his own mortality—or rather his own posthumous status—as Freud writes about a fetish—covering up his own absence *and* creating a memorial to its loss.

: :

If Wright, in his earliest work collected in *Country Music*, can be seen as a hermetic poet of ideogrammic intensity and purity, his late style is baroque: obscurity refracts into transparency, surfaces into depths, the aphoristic into the radiant image, narratives into song. The poet dwells in the indwelling of meditation where the seen and the unseen are appraised and apportioned, but *final* judgment is withheld.

: :

I have been interested in the lyric sequence. The lyric, by its habit, is always looking for the exit the minute it enters a room, always looking for a way to lock the door behind itself just as it has turned around the OPEN sign to those waiting to enter. How can one have both this habit of closure and still have the ongoing-ness of other genres like the essay, the short story, or the novel? One way is to link lyric passages together, allowing each section, at once, to close and open into and onto the next and the next. There is nothing new about this technique—you see it in crowns of sonnets, in lyric groupings like *The Songs of Innocence and Experience*. My habit is most closely aligned, I think, with Ezra Pound's "ideogrammic method," where the juxtapositions are central to the organization.

: :

To write a poem that is a lyric sequence, the sequence itself and the provisional status of each part must be part of the *subject*.

: :

The landscape is a screen onto which one projects.

: :

I do not believe in inspiration. I think that there are times when things do open up before one, as if a gift from some unknown source, but those times are usually because one has prepared oneself for writing—reading, thinking, note-taking, conversation, meditation, brooding, daydreaming, fretting.

: :

I grew up in a tempest of a household, not the magical and comedic realm of Shakespeare's island but a stormy place and more than once on the verge of violence. My parents drank, and their drinking led to arguments, and an argument might send a plate of spaghetti flying across the room or overturn a table. At twelve, with a freedom I took as my own to take, I slipped out of the house and onto my bike and peddled to self-exile at the local library. The aisle straight ahead as I entered was formed on one side by the 700s and on the other by the 800s, so I would grab an armload of art books and another of poetry books to wait out my parents' drama. I passed hours gazing at the great art of the world in reproduction, and reading randomly, and with a hunger, whatever poems to which luck had led me. One poem, Richard Wilbur's "Junk," captivated my imagination at once. Here was a poem made of the "cast-off," the "gimcrack, the "jerrybuilt," which seemed so much a part of the shambles I had left behind at home. Yet, from this hodgepodge, this bric-a-brac detritus, Wilbur weaves something *whole* and bristlingly beautiful (not unlike another poem, Gerard Manly Hopkins' "Pied Beauty," to which my sortilege soon led me).

: :

A journal or diary assumes a privacy that just might be ruptured.

: :

The pleasures of art are the pleasures of ambiguity.

: :

The mastery of an art form, Ezra Pound argued, is the work of a lifetime. Jack Gilbert's small body of work is the work of a master and the work of a lifetime. Bearing a kinship to Pound and to the Greek poet Yannis Ritsos, Gilbert masters both the lyric and epic modes, creating a new modality: the vision and voice of the epic radiant within the confines and subtractions of a lyric utterance. We have not yet attended to his poems with the same intensity he brings to them. I would usually use such words as *austere, minimal,* and *ascetic* to describe Gilbert's poems, stripped as they are of any flourishes and worn down to their stark elements, it seems, by the erosion of time: geologic, mythic, historic, as well as by the time and labor of an individual life. The locus of many of Gilbert's poems is a solitary place, a hillside in Greece, for instance, a landscape composed of dust, moonlight, the distant sound of goat bells. The self that speaks the poems speaks out of isolation, out of exile, stranded, is-landed—a Prospero without his magic. In "Threshing the Fire," he writes: "I would burrow into stone, into iron," as he hears "cicadas on the olive tree rage in brevity." Between brevity and a thousand years is a human life: marooned in time, lived second by second, joy by joy, grief by grief, loss by loss, as a moment forgotten, a moment remembered. In the poem "Adulterated," as in several poems in *The Great Fires*, more and more is added rather than erased, more and more is pulled into the verse's gravity: the sacred and profane, tenderness and cruelty, song and silence, dignity and degradation, distances and intimacies. Which of these adulterate, we might ask ourselves? Which of these offers a falsified vision or a true vision of human baseness and human compassion? Poems are not usually in the business of providing answers. If this poem offers an answer, it balances precariously on the fulcrum of a *therefore*. If this poem offers an answer, it might be glimpsed through the ragged chinks between defeat and glory, nostalgia and bitterness, Gethsemane and Dachau, the sacrifice and the slaughter.

: :

Eve spoke in the tongue of the serpent, which is to say, Eve spoke.

: :

A life spent in words, when the true subject is the unsayable, the untouchable, and the unknowable, leads one either to silence, or to eloquence.

: :

What the dreamer fails to question is the dream.

: :

What I call the *self* is dispersed and yet the *I* is accountable for all its incoherent and fragmentary parts.

: :

I was in love, which is to say I was estranged from reason.

All day saying *No* to Death when it has not even asked a question.

: :

It must have been 1970 or 1971 when I first read "The Love Song of J. Alfred Prufrock" at a large table in the Raytown Public Library. As I thought about the possibility of being a poet—I was eleven or twelve at the time—it seemed that being from Missouri would be a strike against me. Poets lived, I thought, in New York, Paris, or London. Much to my surprise, I kept finding yet another poet who had overcome what seemed to me then as the irremediable handicap of being a Missourian. At this point, I had already checked out and read a couple of times *The Lost Pilot*, a book of poems by a local Kansas City poet, James Tate, which came out in 1967. Then I came upon poems by Marianne Moore, who hailed from Kirkwood, as well as poems by Joplin native Langston Hughes. Somewhere in the search for Missouri poets I read St. Louis native Eliot and the first poem I read of his was "Prufrock." Believe me, I understood little of what I read. Or rather, I should say that I cared little about "meaning" or "understanding." I liked best in poems the surprise of language, the strange image, and the vertigo I felt when language seemed on the verge of nonsense. I like uncertainty, the uncanny way a poem could reveal itself differently each time I return to it. "The Love Song of J. Alfred Prufrock" offered me more than I could have asked for. The epigraph in Italian was the first clue that I would have to let some understanding go if I were to accept the invitation of the poem's first line. I think I read the poem as one might a movie, a medium I was far more fluent in at that time in my life than poetry. The poem proceeded as a montage of images, scenes, and monologs: ". . .the evening is spread out against the sky/ Like a patient etherized upon a table" (lines 2-3). A sickly boy, I had already been anesthetized more than a few times, and the image of the evening spread out against the sky filled me with dis-ease, with dizziness. The jump-cut of the couplet: "In the room the women come and go/Talking of Michelangelo (lines

13-14)" seemed almost comical in its rhyme and reiteration. I found little to like about the star of this movie. Prufrock is fretful, fidgety, and finicky. He is so unlike Michelangelo's heroic, baroque muscular figures. I wondered if somehow I was supposed to supply some answers to his many questions. If so, J. Alfred Prufrock—what a foolish name—was out of luck! A single image from the poem enchanted and entranced me upon my first reading, and if I spent time trying to make sense of something, it was this: "I should have been a pair of ragged claws/ Scuttling across the floors of silent seas" (lines 72-73). The image, coming early in the poem, prepares the reader for the move from the fogged urban maze of streets and claustrophobia-inducing interiors of the poem's earlier stanzas to the seaside at the poem's end. When he says, "I should have been. . ." does he mean "I might as well have been"? Or perhaps, "I wish I had been"? Or perhaps, "I deserve to have been"? Or perhaps, "It is my fate to have been, but that fate was taken from me"? Is it a statement of self-pity? A longing to be not human? Of course, I saw a crustacean—a crab, a lobster—something armored with an exoskeleton—an omnivore, at once a scavenger and a predator. But the self pictured is fragmented—not a whole creature, merely a "pair of ragged claws," bodiless, for a moment, until the next line when it is given legs, "Scuttling across the floors of silent seas." Here in the movie's montage, we go from an extreme close-up on the claws to a sudden long shot that shows the minute arthropod scaled not only against the sea-floor depth, but also against the floors of many seas. I had understood *scuttle* from the context to mean the movement of a crab—a sideways movement in quick burst. I remember looking up *scuttle* upon my first reading of "Prufrock" and wondered if the meaning of deliberately sinking a boat had anything to do with the images of drowning at the poem's end, and wondered just what it meant to "wake" *and* "drown" as a sequence of events. To be left with many questions seemed an appropriate response, I thought then as a boy without answers, to a poem riddled by questions.

: :

The question before me is: "What are your religious or spiritual beliefs, if any, and what effect, if at all, have they had on your work?" The quick and easy answer is that I am certain of nothing. My poems, for the most part, have been a vehicle and a locus for the interrogation and investigation of that uncertainty. Although I am a member of (even a deacon in) The United Church of Christ, a liberal organization doing wonderful work for social justice, I do not honestly believe there is a god or an afterlife. I could say this out loud in my church and no one I think would be surprised or disturbed. What I am attempting to practice as a Christian is how to make sense of Jesus's strange and radical teachings and parables and in doing so learn how to live in *this* world, to be compassionate, to be generous, to be loving, to do more good than damage.

That said, I fear I am like the man in Bob Dylan's song "Ain't Talkin'" from his *Modern Times* album:

> They say prayer has the power to heal
> So pray for me mother
> In the human heart an evil spirit can dwell
> I'm trying to love my neighbor and do good unto others
> But oh, mother, things ain't going well (lines 9-13)

Like Bob Dylan, I once had a "reborn experience." It was a long time ago at a Baptist revival, in what seems now a wholly different life. I say I do not believe in god, yet in *this* life I experienced a mystical encounter that was all at once otherworldly and bodily. To tell such a tale—a supernatural confrontation and transformation, a metamorphosis that belongs to the realm of the mythic—is to provoke your listener's disbelief. One may as well confess to hearing voices, to seeing ghosts. Did such a thing happen? How has the attempt to give language to the mystery of such an experience blurred or distorted it? Clarified it? Turned it to mere story? Into fragmented figures and images? After giving a reading from my collection, *Apocrypha*, the first of my books to actively meditate upon that experience and the mythic constructs of the Gospels, an audience member, asking a similar question to the one at the start of this essay, prefaced the question with the statement, "You seem unabashed about your religious belief . . ." suggesting, of course, that one might be, or more likely, one ought to be abashed to traffic at such hocus-pocus. Perhaps I should have been. Perhaps I should be. But I am not. Poetry is a meditative space where I suspend conclusion, where I can avoid final thoughts, where I can attempt what John Keats calls *negative capability*, where one "is capable of being in uncertainties, Mysteries, doubts, without any irritable reaching after fact and reason"(277).

My poems find themselves on the tight rope between faith and doubt, between the mystical and the practical, between the enumeration of things seen and the enumeration of those things beyond our senses. I take solace in the contradictory stories of the canonical and non-canonical gospels. In *this* world, I do what I can to follow Jesus's admonitions to help feed the hungry, to give a drink to the thirsty. My efforts are small and the participation in and affiliation with a church helps multiply, amplify, and focus those small deeds. As Dylan says, "I'm trying to love my neighbor and do good unto others." Wallace Stevens, whose poetry is a lifelong search for an apt replacement for the gods and scriptures says, "The final belief is to believe in a fiction, which you know to be a fiction, there being nothing else. The exquisite truth is to know that it is a fiction and that you believe in it willingly" (189). I believe it willingly with all the doubt in the world.

: :

I imagine as my ideal reader a reader who loves all the poets I love, but even more so.

: :

How to make a *new* art without the hygienic impulse to sterilize, to clean up the litter and mess of the prior art? Why is each *avant garde* as reactionary as it is revolutionary?

: :

Teaching is a blessing, and I put a great deal of energy and thought into it. I cannot imagine a better way to spend my time or earn a living. I have always written with my students, at-tempting the same prompts and exercises (often generated by the students) that the students are attempting. I try to model for them what I believe: that we practice poetry. Once we are fluent at x, y, and z, it is time to attempt a, b, and c. We have learned as well that originality is not novelty, but what one can do to promote and/or rebel against the conventions of an art form in a given moment in history. That is to say, originality is found in the particular, and often peculiar, ways an individual poet riffs on all that has come before her.

20 A Concordance of Silence

The small child learns a new gesture: an upright index finger to the lips.

: :

"In short, we must consider speech before it is spoken, the background of silence that does not cease to surround it and without which it would say nothing. Or to put the matter another way, we must uncover the threads of silence that speech is mixed together with" (241). —Maurice Merleau-Ponty

: :

After my father died, I would wake at night and go to the window. My father would be there standing in the ruined garden beneath winter rain. His mouth moved as if around words but said nothing I could hear. Straining to hear, I heard the rain, as it turned to ice, tick against the window.

: :

Silence in music is notated as a *rest*. An interval of silence. What is it to endure the duration of silence?

: :

"Of the four characteristics of the material of music, duration, that is time length, is the most fundamental. Silence cannot be heard in terms of pitch or harmony: it is heard in terms of time length.(77)" —John Cage

: :

The silence of the caesura *is*, yet is outside the measure of the poem's meter.

To teach is to live inside an awkward silence. The silence is not awkward, but the fact that no one dares interrupt it is.

Submerged in the depth of a cave, I have turned out the flashlight and found myself in total darkness. My hand held an inch from my face had no visible presence. But there was no silence: the slow drip from stalactite to stalagmite, the mechanics and rasp of my breathing, the pumped rush of my blood inside my head.

The poet, like the depressive, is often mired in the silence of speechlessness and unsayability.

The mime's silence is not uncanny, but the exaggerated accuracy of the mime's gestures are.

"Not speaking and speaking are both human ways of being in the world, and there are kinds and grades of each. There is the dumb silence of slumber or apathy; the sober silence that goes with a solemn animal face; the fertile silence of awareness, pasturing the soul, whence emerge new thoughts; the alive silence of alert perception, ready to say, "This... this..."; the musical silence that accompanies absorbed activity; the silence of listening to another speak, catching the drift and helping him be clear; the noisy silence of resentment and self-recrimination, loud and subvocal speech but sullen to say it; baffled silence; the silence of peaceful accord with other persons or communion with the cosmos" (15). —Paul Goodman

: :

Shush, I repeat to hush the infant, the *sh, sh, sh,* losing its vowel over time, as the child calms, as her body slacks into sleep—in her quiet she seems suddenly under the pull of gravity, heavier in my arms, though she barely weighs a thing—her cries having transmuted to hiccupy breaths, then at last to silence; her small chest lifting, lowering. *Sh, sh, sh,* I say under my breath as I rock the child in my arms. *Shush,* I say, but only to soothe myself.

: :

Silent prayer. Silent treatment. Silent letter. Silent partner. The broken silence. The silent emptiness of an unstruck bell. The measured silence between lightning and thunder. Shelf after shelf, room after room of books read silently.

: :

Silence as perfection: the unmarred, unmarked. Is the perfect poem one that is beyond words? Has done away with words?

: :

"'Silence' never ceases to imply its opposite and to depend on its presence: just as there can't be 'up' without 'down' or 'left' without 'right,' so one must acknowledge a surrounding environment of sound or language in order to recognize silence … A genuine emptiness, a pure silence is not feasible— either conceptually or in fact. If only because the artwork exists in a world furnished with many other things, the artist who creates silence or emptiness must produce something dialectical: a full void, an enriching emptiness, a resonating or eloquent silence. Silence remains, inescapably, a form of speech (in many instances, of complaint or indictment) and an element in a dialogue" (292). —Susan Sontag

: :

I am losing my hearing. I should take action. I have worn glasses since I was twelve. Why am I vain about a hearing aid? I tend to guess at what I think someone has said to me these days. I mishear. I misapprehend. It is as if everyone (and this is when I can *almost* hear them) is speaking in malapropisms. The rest of the time what I hear could have been written by way of the *N+7 procedure*, which I would mishear as "endless heaven precedes her."

: :

"It is the nature of a word to reveal what is hidden. The word that is hidden still sparkles in the darkness and whispers in the silence." —Meister Eckhart (5)

: :

To hear the silence I try several experiments. I bracket the silence with sound. I cross out what has been written on either side of the silence, but the crossing out just calls more attention to the words crossed-out. I put nothing inside the parentheses and listen. I try not to make a sound, and when I do, I imagine that what came before was the *silence*.

: :

Paintings are, of course, silent, but in Giorgio Morandi's still-lifes, one senses the gathering and assertion of silence, as if each object over a long time has been dusted with silence, a silence that accumulates as snow might, and whatever sound might rise from the stilled tabletop has been buried. In Whistler's *nocturnes*, on the other hand, one senses the night sounds, sounds muted and baffled by fog: dislocated as they enlarge and distort the distances. The silence of de Chirico's torqued cityscapes is like the silence of a stage set—the curtain has opened. The theater's seats are empty. The dressing rooms are unoccupied; the stagehand is already at home in bed submerged in a dreamless sleep. On the final backdrop, a train departs in the distance. It is a painting of a train and is, of course, silent. From this distance, one sees steam released as a puff from the whistle before one hears it.

: :

Without you even the silence is depleted. Shadows, out of proportion to their objects, gather like standing water in the shallows. I survey and measure and find vacancy.

: :

"I am the silence that is incomprehensible." (298) —*The Thunder, Perfect Mind*

: :

Submerged in silence.
Conjured by silence.
Surrounded by silence.
Detached from silence.
Accompanied by silence.
Resigned to silence.
Attended by silence.
Adrift on silence.
Detained by silence.
Silent within silence.

: :

"Silence contains everything in itself. It is not waiting for anything, it is always wholly present in itself and it completely fills out the space in which it appears." —Max Picard, *The World of Silence* (17)

: :

After my father died, I would wake at night and go to the window. My father would be there standing in the ruined garden beneath winter rain. His mouth moved as if around words but said nothing I could hear. Silently, the rain-soaked window turned opaque with ice.

: :

As is often thcase, silence has the final word.

Works Cited

Alter, Robert ed. Kermode, Frank ed. *The Literary Guide to the Bible.* Harvard UP, 1987.

Ammons, A. R. *Collected Poems 1951-1971.* W.W. Norton and Company, 1972.

Bates, Milton J. *Wallace Stevens Opus Posthumous: Poems, Plays. Prose.* Alfred A. Knopf, 1989.

Baudelaire, Charles. *The Painters of Modern Life.* Translated by Jonathan Mane. Phaidon Press, 1995.

Buckley, Vincent. *Poetry and the Sacred.* Chatto and Windus, 1968.

Cairns, Craig *Associationism and the Literary Imagination.* Edinburg UP, 2007.

Chaung Tsu. *The Inner Chapters.* Translated by David Hinton, Counterpoint, 2014.

Coffin, Charles M. *The Complete Poetry and Selected Prose of John Donne.* Modern Library, 1952.

Der Hummel uber Berlin. Dir. Wim Wenders. Road Movies Filmproduktion and Argos Films, 1987.

Eliot, T. S. *Collected Poems 1909-1935.* Harcourt, Brace and Company, 1936.

—. *George Herbert.* Longman, 1962.

—. *Selected Prose.* Harcourt, Inc. 1975.

Eliot, Valerie, ed. John Haffenden ed. *The Letters of T. S. Eliot: Volume 5, 1930–1931.* Yale UP, 2015.

Frank, Joseph. *The Idea of Spatial Form.* Rutgers UP, 1991.

Freedberg, Daniel. *The Power of Images: Studies in the History and Theory of Response.* U of Chicago P, 1989.

Fox, Matthew. *Meister Eckhart.* New World Library, 2014.

Frost, Robert. *Frost: Collected Poems, Prose, and Plays*. Library of America, 1995.

Gardner, W. H. ed. N. H. MacKenzie ed. *The Poems of Gerard Manley Hopkins*. Oxford UP, 1967.

Garrels, Gary, et al. *Plane Image: A Brice Marden Retrospective*. Museum of Modern Art, 2006.

Gioia, Dana ed. William Logan ed. *Certain Solitudes: On the Poetry of Donald Justice*. U of Arkansas P, 1997.

Goodman, Paul. *Speaking and Language: Defence of Poetry*. Random House, 1971.

Jay, Martin. *Force Fields: Between Intellectual History and Cultural Critique*. Routledge, 1993.

Johnson, Thomas H. ed. *The Complete Poems of Emily Dickinson*. Little Brown. 1960.

---. *The Letters of Emily Dickinson*. Harvard UP, 1986.

Joyce, James. *Stephen Hero*. New Directions, 1944.

Justice, Donald. *Collected Poems*. Alfred A. Knopf, 2004.

---. *Platonic Scripts*. U of Michigan P, 1984.

---. *Oblivion: On Writers and Writing*. Storyline Press, 1998.

Kostelanetz, Richard. ed. *John Cage: An Anthology*. Da Capo, 1970.

Levis, Larry. *Winter Stars*. U of Pittsburg P, 1985.

Lorca, Federico Garcia. *In Search of Duende*. Translated by Christopher Maurer. New Directions, 1998.

Merwin, W. S. *The Rain in the Trees*. Alfred A. Knopf, 1988.

Miller, Nicholas Andrew. *Modernism, Ireland and The Erotics of Memory*. Cambridge UP, 2002.

Monteiro, George. *Robert Frost and the New England Resnaissance*. UP of Kentucky. 1988.

O'Connor, Flannery. *Mystery and Manners*. Farrar, Straus and Giroux, 1970.

Picard, Max. *The World of Silence*. Eighth Day Press, 2002.

Roberts, Adam, ed. *Coleridge: Lectures on Shakespeare (1811-1819)*. Edinburgh UP, 2016.

Robinson, James M. ed. *The Nag Hammadi Library*. Harper and Row, 1988.

Santayana, George. *Interpretations of Poetry and Religion*. Charles Scribner's Sons, 1900.

—. *The Idea of Christ in the Gospels or God in Man.* Charles Scribner's Sons, 1946.

Scudder, Horace. *The Complete Poetical Works and Letters of John Keats.* Boston, Riverside Press, 1899.

Sontag, Susan, *Essays of the 1960s and 70s.* Library of America, 2013.

Stevens, Wallace, *The Collected Poems of Wallace Stevens.* Alfred A. Knopf, 1975.

Stravinsky, Igor. *Poetics of Music in the Form of Six Lessons.* Harvard UP, 1942.

Toadvine, Ted ed. Leonard Lawlor ed. *The Merleau-Ponty Reader.* Northwestern UP, 2007.

Weil, Simone. *Gravity and Grace.* Routledge, 1952.

Woolf, Virginia. *Moments of Being.* Harcourt Brace Javanovich, 1976.

Wordsworth, William, *The Prelude: A Parallel Text.* Penguin, 1996.

About the Author

Eric Pankey is the author of ten previous collections of poetry, including most recently *Alias: Prose Poems*. *Dismantling the Angel* (2014) received the New Measure Poetry Prize. His work has been supported by fellowships from the Ingram Merrill Foundation, The National Endowment for the Arts, the Brown Foundation, and the John Simon Guggenheim Memorial Foundation. He is Professor of English and the Heritage Chair in Writing at George Mason University in Fairfax, Virginia, where he teaches in the MFA and BFA programs in Creative Writing.

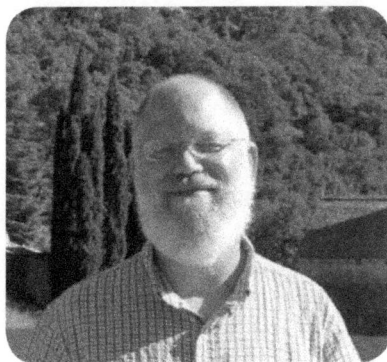

Photograph of Eric Pankey by a friendly tourist.

www.ingramcontent.com/pod-product-compliance
Lightning Source LLC
Chambersburg PA
CBHW022035090426
42741CB00007B/1078